EAST COAST VICTORIANS

EAST COAST VICTORIANS

Castles & Cottages

Kenneth Naversen

Beautiful America Publishing Company©
P.O. Box 646
Wilsonville, OR 97070

Design: Michael Brugman
Typesetting: Oregon Typesetting
Printing: Hong Kong
First Edition: August, 1990

Library of Congress Cataloging-in-Publication Data

Naversen, Kenneth, 1944-
    East Coast Victorians: Castles & Cottages

    Includes bibliographical references and index.
    1. Architecture, Domestic—Atlantic Coast (U.S.)
2. Architecture, Victorian—Atlantic Coast (U.S.)
I. Title.
NA7208.7.N38 1990
728'.0974—dc20   90-860 CIP

ISBN: 0-89802-550-8 (paper)

ISBN: 0-89802-552-4 (cloth)

To The Colonel & Mrs.

Table of Contents

Introduction

A taste for rural improvements of every description is advancing silently, but with great rapidity in this country. While yet in the far west the pioneer constructs his rude hut of logs for a dwelling, and sweeps away with his axe the lofty forest trees that encumber the ground, in the older portions of the Union, bordering the Atlantic, we are surrounded by all the luxuries and refinements that belong to an old and long established country. Within the last ten years, especially, the evidence of the growing wealth and prosperity of our citizens have become apparent in the great increase of elegant cottages and villa residences on the banks of our noble rivers, along our rich valleys, and wherever nature seems to invite us by her rich and varied charms.

Thus, in graceful, midcentury prose, Andrew Jackson Downing, landscape gardener and architectural tastemaker, summarized the state of American domestic architecture at the beginning of the 1840s. He was writing, though he didn't know it, at the dawn of a new age. It had begun in 1837 when an eighteen-year-old princess became Queen of the United Kingdoms of England and Ireland, and it ended, along with her reign, in 1901. We know it today as the Victorian era: sixty-odd years during which the United States transformed itself from a youthful, idealistic, largely rural republic into a mature industrial nation which straddled an entire continent.

An enumeration of some of the events that occurred during this remarkable period is enough to suggest how extensive this transformation was. The Mexican War and the California gold rush, the Civil War, the advent of railroads and Robber Barons, the rise of industrialization, a demographic shift from rural to urban, the arrival of an unprecedented tide of immigrants from Europe—all these left a dramatic impress on the country.

Along with these major events, quieter developments in the nation's cultural history were also taking place. Among them was the rise of the sundry architectural modes that dominated American housing in the last half of the nineteenth century—the styles we know today as Victorian.

This varied group ranged from the quaint Gothic Revival of Downing's day to the flamboyant Queen Anne that held sway at the end of the century. It comprised modish imports like the refined Italianate and haughty French Second Empire as well as home-grown potatoes such as the Stick and Shingle styles. And it also included oddities like the Octagon house and several species of "Oriental" villa. Victorian houses might be the work of well-known architects or of anonymous carpenter-builders. In scale they might vary from

diminutive cottages to enormous mansions. And they could assume any shape from formal town house to rambling country villa.

All in all, the domestic architecture of the era constituted a mixed bag that has challenged the ingenuity of twentieth-century taxonomists. But for all their diversity, Victorian houses share certain qualities that distinguish them from both their predecessors and successors.

For one thing, they were generally enamored of ornament. The exact form of decoration varied from style to style, but the tendency to make use of it remained constant throughout the era. Elaborate bargeboards and flat-cut gingerbread marked the Gothic Revival; carved lintels and brackets, the Italianate; shingles and lathe-turned spindlework, the Queen Anne. The list could go on, but suffice it to say that even modest houses were partial to decoration in the late nineteenth century, and the bolder ones were florid in the extreme.

Another characteristic of the Victorian house was its proclivity to sprout fanciful extensions of all sorts. Towers, turrets, rambling wings, bay windows, wraparound porches, gazebos, cupolas, belvederes, pinnacles, and high-flying chimney stacks were some of the means by which the houses of the era achieved picturesque form—and in the process broke free of the boxy shapes that had imprisoned their ancestors.

A taste for ornament and the picturesque, however, is only part of what makes a house Victorian. Another necessary ingredient is a sense of drama and whimsy, a certain spirit of make believe and let's pretend. Victorian houses were a little like children dressing up in costumes from long ago and far away. By donning the appropriate architectural trappings, they sought to evoke the appearance and—more importantly—the spirit of the romantic past and exotic present.

This sense of theatre was a reflection of the profound romanticism of the nineteenth century, and more than anything else it separates the architecture of the period from that of the classical and the modern eras. It explains why Victorian houses often resembled Medieval castles, French chateaux, Gothic cottages, Persian villas, and a host of other models, some real, some merely fanciful. Often, in fact, they found inspiration in sources that were as much literary as architectural—hence all the castellated parapets, nooks, crannies, and tower hideaways right out of Sir Walter Scott.

In its American beginnings the new picturesque architecture was exclusively an East Coast phenomenon. As the most established and civilized section of the country, the East was the natural fount of the architectural ideas that were to dominate the United States for the next half-century.

However, when Downing penned the preface to his *Treatise on the Theory and Practice of Landscape Gardening Adapted to North America* (1841), the United States extended from the Atlantic to the Mississippi and not much beyond. A few American trappers, missionaries, and settlers had made inroads in the far west, but Mexico still held Texas and California, and Great Britain was in nominal possession of the Oregon Territory. While John Chapman was planting apple seedlings in the Old Northwest and Pio Pico, governor of California, was just beginning to worry out loud about the perfidious Yankees who had lately begun trickling over the Sierras, Gothic castles and cottages were rising on the Hudson.

If the fount of the new architecture was the Eastern Seaboard, its wellsprings lay in England where the ideals of the romantic and picturesque movements had coalesced in the works of writers like John Claudius Loudon, Humphry Repton, and John Ruskin. In adapting their ideas for an American audience and the American landscape, A.J. Downing (1815-1852) played a key role.

Born in Newburgh, New York, a small town on the Hudson, Downing was the son of a nurseryman and acquired a keen knowledge of fruit trees, ornamental gardening, and landscaping in the very process of growing up. His practical education was supplemented by extensive reading, and his good looks and considerable charm won him important social connections, which, no doubt, were bolstered by his marriage to Carolyn de Windt, a niece of John Quincy Adams.

Not content merely to retrace his father's footsteps, Downing, once grown, put his hand to writing and won quick success with his *Treatise*. A particularly favorable response to the section on rural architecture led him to produce *Cottage Residences* (1842), and *The Architecture of Country Houses* (1850). Meanwhile he had begun editing a magazine, *The Horticulturist*, which provided him for six years with a continuing forum for advancing his ideas on "rural art and rural taste."

The broad acceptance of picturesque architecture in America was stimulated by Downing's enormously influential books, each of which was reprinted many times in the nineteenth century. Houses explicitly based on the designs illustrated in these works can still be found in many parts of the country. But Downing's ideas had a far more lasting effect than any individual house plan he may have published.

In general he mirrored the agrarian ideals of his age—the virtues of rural life and the importance of the single-family home—and the egalitarian spirit of his young country. Good architecture, he felt, was not the exclusive province of the wealthy: in a republic, even a humble cottage, rightly designed and constructed, could aspire to the station of art.

One consistent theme in his writings was the need for "truthfulness" in architecture. Houses, he believed, should be honest in presenting themselves to the world. A wooden house should not pretend to be of stone, and a cottage should not purport to be a castle. This ideal extended also to the location of a house and to its owner. An honest dwelling should complement its surroundings, and it should also be expressive of—or at least consistent with—the character and lifestyle of its occupant. Downing's examples include the sturdy farmer in his Gothic cottage and the aristocratic planter in his Italian villa. He warned against castles, however. ". . .unless there is something of the castle in the man," he wrote, "it is very likely. . .to dwarf him to the stature of a mouse."

Downing's strong personal preference for the Gothic Revival style may have had to do with his rearing on the banks of the Hudson. A mythopoeic body of water even in his day, it had already begun to spawn its own ghosts and mysteries.

Nathaniel Hawthorne had complained of ". . .the difficulty of writing a romance about a country where there is no shadow, no antiquity, no mystery, no picturesque and gloomy wrong, nor anything but a commonplace prosperity in broad and simple daylight. . . ." But then Hawthorne lived in prim New England. Washington Irving, who, like Downing, abided by the Hudson, apparently had little trouble conjuring up headless horsemen and sleeping Dutchmen to people its misty, purple-hued banks. In addition, the river was soon to inspire new movements: an entire school of painters whose creations exuded just the sort of atmospheric gloom that Hawthorne longed for, along with an architectural style that came to be known as Hudson River Gothic.

So Downing, too, may have been affected by some spirit that inhabited the river. In any case, he thought the whitewashed Greek Revival temple-style houses that had sprung up along its lower reaches were singularly inappropriate for such a moody, romantic setting. In their stead he recommended cottages in the English or rural Gothic style.

Nicholas Pevsner has observed that the main difference between the Greek and Gothic Revivals is that the former was "correct" and that the latter was not. He was speaking of Europe, but the observation is also and particularly appropriate to the United States where firsthand knowledge of Gothic architecture was slight. Relatively few books had been published on the subject on either side of the Atlantic. And America, unlike Europe, had no venerable old castles and cathedrals and only a handful of Gothic cottages from which to draw inspiration. This dearth of models left a lot of room for imaginative invention on the part of builders and architects.

Houses in the American Carpenter's Gothic tradition imitated, in wood, forms and structures that had originally been executed in stone. In their purest form they were frame cottages with board-and-batten siding, pointed-arch windows, and steep gables decorated with ornamental bargeboards. Even when laid out in plans of balanced symmetry, they were "picturesque" and irregular by comparison with Greek or Colonial houses. This, in Downing's view, made them more appropriate for the rugged rural environment of the New World. To further enhance this harmony he recommended that they be painted in dark and somber hues—greens and earth tones—the colors of nature. White, the color of Greek classicism, was singled out as especially to be avoided.

In the generation immediately preceding the Civil War, the principal architect of the Gothic Revival in America was Alexander Jackson Davis (1803-1892). His picturesque conceptions strongly influenced Downing, and it was his generally uncredited hand that created many of the drawings that illustrated the latter's books and articles.

A dozen years older than Downing, Davis had worked as a printer and dabbled in the theatre before reaching a decision to make a career of painting. At the suggestion of Rembrandt Peale, a noted artist of the day, he became an architectural illustrator, an occupation which soon led him to begin designing buildings of his own. In the early 1830s his exquisite draughtmanship and flair for design won him a partnership with Ithiel Town, the outstanding Greek Revivalist of the period. But by the end of the decade Davis had hung up his own shingle and was conducting a highly successful architectural practice.

Meanwhile, he had developed a strong preference for the Gothic Revival. His *Rural Residences* (1838) was the first American book to explore the possibilities of the country Gothic style. This folio of drawings never achieved wide distribution, but it was nonetheless important both in engendering a taste for picturesque architecture in the United States and in advertising Davis' talents. Although the bulk of his work was executed in New York state, he was also in demand in New England and Virginia, and houses based on his

designs can be found as far afield as Ohio and even Oregon.

Another popular building style in the early Victorian period was the Italianate. The term comprises both formal, symmetrical houses, which are sometimes designated as Tuscan, and irregular villas that are supposed to be based on the vernacular farmhouses of the Campagna. Since most of the Italianate houses built in the United states were modeled after English interpretations of Italian originals, however, their resemblance to any actual dwelling in Italy was probably slight. Edith Wharton implied as much in *The Age of Innocence* when she wrote: "People had always been told that the house. . .was an Italian villa. Those who had never been to Italy believed it; so did some who had."

In general the style was characterized by flat or low-pitched roofs with overhanging eaves supported by carved ornamental brackets. Windows were usually round headed or segmental arched, and there was often a corner tower or—alternatively—a cupola set at the apex of the roof. Some houses in the Italian villa style were remarkably free in plan, with extended wings and bays that liberated the American house for the first time from the rectangular box shape of its Colonial and Classical past.

Although Downing preferred the Gothic Revival style for cottages, he was also fond of the Italianate and considered it particularly appropriate for the country homes of sophisticated men of the world. He also noted that it was well suited to the climate of the South, where indeed it flourished to a degree that Gothic Revival—despite some interesting exceptions—never did.

For many Dixie planters Italianate dwellings were just a step away from the Greek-inspired plantation houses that had dominated the South earlier in the century. The formal Tuscan mode, in particular, had much the same aristocratic demeanor as those older houses, and it was probably more livable.

But the Italianate style was popular in the North, too. By the 1860s it had largely supplanted the Gothic, at least partly because it was more adaptable to the constraints of city lots. In the building booms that bracketed the Civil War, Italianate houses proliferated, appearing in the suburbs as compressed versions of expansive country villas and in the city as rowhouses newly adorned with ornamental details derived from the Italian Renaissance.

• • • • •

Andrew Jackson Downing died at the age of thirty-seven, the untimely victim of a fire aboard a Hudson River steamer that had entered into an impromptu and imprudent race with another riverboat. He was last seen alive throwing wooden deck chairs over the side to fellow passengers foundering in the waters below. Though his career was cut short, his books remained influential for at least a generation after his death, and many of the ideas he promoted—in particular the virtues of suburban living and the ideal of the single-family home—are still with us today.

After his demise, his publisher, Luther Tucker, saw the writing on the wall and lost no time in commending *The Horticulturist*, to others' hands. His instincts were sure, for though the magazine stayed in print until the 1870s, it never again matched the early success it had enjoyed under Downing.

The Horticulturist, however, was only one of a number of periodicals that fostered the spread of architectural ideas during the Victorian era. Another important and even more widely-read source was the brain child of the Philadelphia publisher Louis A. Godey. *Godey's Lady's Book*, a national monthly, was the nineteenth-century forerunner of such popular women's magazines as *Ladies' Home Journal, Redbook*, and perhaps even *Ms*, inasmuch as its editors were all women. Its basic strategy was to be informative and authoritative on all matters that might be of interest to "intelligent, discerning ladies." And in this it was highly successful from 1830 until 1898—nearly seventy years. In each issue literature, poetry, popular science, and history vied with recipes and dress patterns for the reader's attention. The formula was evidently successful, for Godey's achieved a circulation of 130,000 before the Civil War and a half million by the late 1860s.

In September 1846—just a month after Downing began editing *The Horticulturist* — Godey's issued a sort of manifesto in which it declared itself foursquare on the side of "beautiful architecture." It also promised to publish a new house plan each month, and—true to its word—presented about 450 designs over the next half century. In the process, it helped establish the reputations of such notable architects as Samuel Sloan, Isaac Hobbs, and Theophilus P. Chandler, each of whom reigned for a decade or so as the journal's favorite designer.

That both *Godey's* and *The Horticulturist* should simultaneously begin to advocate "cottage architecture" as an ideal for American housing is symptomatic of the changes that were taking place in the country at mid-century. The evolving nation was beginning to miss its water even as the well ran dry. In the 1850s America was already becoming increasingly urban and industrial, and—like England a half century earlier—was beginning to romanticize its fading village and country life. This was especially true of those city dwellers who, having grown up in the country, were inclined to get a bit misty about the old family homestead. Henry Williams, who edited *The Horticulturist* some years after Downing's death, played to this crowd in a schmaltzy editorial.

Many have been born and brought up in a village, who have yet enjoyed city life for many years. Yet there has never been a day in the history of their eventful careers but they have looked back with longing to the dear old village home, 'father's cottage'. . . All these reminiscences of cottage life touch a chord in the breast of many who are absent from them and lead us to believe that the real beauty and charm of rural life never have been, and never will be, described.

Which may explain why Gothic cottages and Italianate villas continued to be built in parts of the country long after they had gone out of style. Whether constructed to serve as bona fide farmhouses or ornamental summer cottages, they represented the old dream and served to palliate the sometimes painful changes that America was experiencing in the late nineteenth century.

There were those, of course, who were scarcely aware that change of any sort was afoot. As Edmund Wilson put it, "The old mansions with their vast tracts of land enabled their masters to live in an independent state of dream quite aloof from the preoccupations of the growing industrial cities."

He was referring to upstate New York, where remnants of the Dutch Patroon system lingered on even after the turn of the century. But the comment is equally true of the plantation South and of some other areas of the country as well. After the Civil War, however, change became less easy to ignore anywhere in the United States. The postwar years witnessed a dramatic transformation of America's economy, her social class system, and her built environment.

While the South was coping with reconstruction, the North, thanks to the prodigious growth of industry, railroads, shipping, and banking, was prospering as never before. It goes without saying that the new wealth was not divided proportionately among the population, but the extent of the disparity between rich and poor that began to occur in this era was remarkable. As millionaires became common, the country's once-vaunted egalitarianism began to fade into myth.

Architecturally the new affluence found expression in the French Second Empire style which Louis Napoleon and Baron Haussmann had employed when they rebuilt Paris in the late 1850s. Even before the Civil War the style had made a few isolated appearances in the United States, but it did not become truly popular until the flood of Americans who had set off on the grand tour in the postwar era returned with sophisticated ideas about what their own homes should look like. In contrast to the rustic cottages of Downing and Davis, the French style radiated an aura of modernity and elegance that perfectly mirrored the opulence of the times.

As in the case of Italianate houses, most Second Empire dwellings erected in America were based on English interpretations of French originals and may have lost something in the translation. Many of the secondary details—window dressings, cornice brackets, and so forth—hardly differed from Italianate ornament. The chief feature that distinguished the French style was a distinctive two-sloped mansard roof. Since a mansard adds nearly as much space to a structure as an additional story, it had been adopted in Paris as a way of bypassing zoning restrictions that limited buildings to six floors. In the United States, however, it soon became a mark of distinction. A mansard roof atop a house indicated that its owner was—or wished to be—wealthy, sophisticated, and well traveled.

As signaled by the irreverent nickname "General Grant style," the pretentious side of the Second Empire was already apparent in the Victorian era. With the passage of time it became even more obvious. Those Second Empire mansions that survived into the twentieth century came to be regarded as the ultimate white elephants, perfect symbols of the preposterous ostentation and lapsed taste of the 1860s and '70s. It was not by accident that the cartoonist Charles Adams chose precisely such a mansion to house his fictional Adams Family. It is only recently that people have once again been able to look at the breed with some semblance of neutrality.

The financial troubles that began in the early 1870s spelled a temporary end to Second-Empire extravagance, and by end of the decade when the general euphoria began to return, new architectural modes had gained ascendancy. Some of the houses that arose during this period looked like nothing so much as a new incarnation of the Gothic Revival style. Contemporary architects, in fact, sometimes referred to them as "Modern Gothic." In general, they were tall and angular and had steep-pitched roofs and elaborate gable trusses. In addition many of them were decorated with a distinctive type of ornament which included thin vertical battens and stylized cross braces. These were the houses of the so-called "Stick style."

Vincent Scully, Jr., who coined the term, pointed out that this characteristic patterning was an extension of the board-and-batten tradition of the Gothic Revival and an echo of the half-timbered houses of the Tudor period. He also suggested that stick-work decoration signaled a renewal of interest in the ideals of structural honesty that had been partly submerged during America's flirtation with the Second Empire. The stylized posts, beams, and braces that adorned the outer skin of the structure mirrored the frame skeleton that actually supported it.

Related to the Stick style was a decorative mode called "Eastlake." The term originally derived from the work of the English architect and designer Charles Locke Eastlake (1836-1908), whose *Hints on Household Taste* (1872) illustrated interiors decorated with carved and incised designs, linear stripping, and rows of knob-like projections. However, in the United States—especially in uninhibited San Francisco—details of this sort soon began appearing on the exteriors of buildings as well. This style came to be known as "Eastlake," much to the discomfiture of its eponym. In 1882 *The California Architect and Building News* quoted the Englishman as follows:

> I now find, to my amazement, that there exists, on the other side of the Atlantic, an "Eastlake style" of architecture, which, judging from the specimens I have seen illustrated, may be said to burlesque such doctrines of art as I have ventured to maintain . . . I feel greatly flattered by the popularity which my books have attained in America, but I regret that their author's name should be associated there with a phase of taste in architecture and industrial art with which I can have no real sympathy and which, by all accounts, seems to be extravagant and bizarre.

As Marcus Whiffen has pointed out, Eastlake ornament differed from earlier flat-cut gingerbread in that it was the product not of the saw but rather of chisels, knives, and gouges—the latter often used in conjunction with steam-powered milling machines. The incised panels, lathe-turned posts, spindles, and rows of projecting knobs that these tools produced were often applied to houses in the Stick and Queen Anne styles. Houses with a plethora of such ornament, however, are often simply called "Eastlake."

If the stick style was Gothic at root, it was also part of a stylistic branch that led to the Queen Anne. Again the name is confusing, and was recognized as such even when it was new. "Queen Anne," wrote a Victorian architectural commentator, "is a comprehensive name which has been made to cover a multitude of incongruities, including, indeed, the bulk of recent work which otherwise defies description."

The term seems to have been used initially to describe several houses that were erected as part of the British pavilion at the American Centennial Exposition of 1876. And it is supposed to have historic roots in some box-like, eighteenth-century houses that were popular during the reign of Queen Anne of England. The Victorian Queen Anne house however, was thoroughly nineteenth century in tone; and in the United States it took on a whole new life. The American version was typically an extended, hipped-roof, towered affair covered with a range of surface ornament which might include stick-work, shingles, and Eastlake sunbursts.

Not everyone liked such houses of course. The architect John Wellborn

Root used to refer to the Queen Anne as the "Tubercular Style," and—in reference to its penchant for surface ornament—noted that "Its eruptive tendencies manifest themselves in all sorts of things, from wens to carbuncles and ringworms."

Nonetheless, as John Maas has pointed out, this "historicizing flummery. . .covered a very sound body. . .planned from the inside out." Indeed, in its layout and interior planning the late Victorian house anticipated the concept of "organic architecture" that Frank Lloyd Wright promulgated early in the twentieth century. Once building was liberated from the restrictions of the box, architects became free to explore the logic of function in creating a design.

Much of this new freedom was due to the development of the balloon frame, an innovative building technique that has been hailed as the first genuine American contribution to the science of architecture. The original use of the new system is credited to a Yankee named Augustine Taylor who lived in the Chicago area in the 1840s. For the heavy posts and beams that had supported wooden houses ever since medieval times, he substituted numerous two-by-fours which he tied together with nails and diagonal cross-braces. The result was a structural framework that was amazingly strong, easy to construct, and graciously amenable to departures from tradition.

Thanks to the balloon frame—which in turn owed to the advent of inexpensive, machine-produced nails—interior layouts became more logical and livable in the late nineteenth century. The four-pens-and-a-passage plan common in Greek and Gothic Revival homes gave way to a freer interior organization which in turn determined the outer shape of the house. The new framing technique made it possible to place doors, windows, and entire wings where they were most needed. And it also encouraged builders to add such typically Victorian extensions as bays and towers to a structure. What is more, it made it possible for even inexperienced builders to erect more complicated and sophisticated houses than would have been possible for them in the past.

Despite these technical advances, however, architectural design in the late Victorian period was often timid, hidebound, and conservative. In the main this was due to emotional links that tied the houses of the day to the ideals of the past.

In the South, particularly, new developments in architecture were slow to be accepted. Part of the reason was the genuine poverty of many parts of the region, but another part has the distinct taste of sour grapes. J.C. Furnas recalls a local lady telling him that Charleston's poverty after the Civil War had at least spared it "the Gingerbread horrors" that afflicted other cities in

the same period—a plausible explanation for the dearth of Victoriana in town, but a disingenuous one. In fact, Charleston wasn't so much impoverished as it was indisposed to accept what it saw as Yankee intrusions on its culture.

To a lesser degree the same attitude informed the rest of the South as well. While its population clung to the myth of a lost Eden symbolized architecturally by the Greek Revival plantation house, the region failed to keep abreast of the latest architectural fashions in the postwar era. This was especially true in the Tidewater, but even in the Piedmont, which was generally more accepting of new trends, late-nineteenth-century dwellings often took on the prim, classical demeanor of the manor houses of the antebellum period. That southern houses tended to be painted white, however, seems to have been due as much to the searing heat of summer as to any allegiance to tradition.

Architectural conservatism was not confined to the South, of course. New England, too, was generally resistant to the more ebullient of the Victorian styles, and elsewhere in the North there were other pockets of resistance.

As George E. Thomas notes in his study of Cape May, New Jersey, for example, the town remained ostensibly ignorant of the latest architectural trends throughout the latter half of the nineteenth century. Though a series of major fires gave Cape May frequent opportunities to adopt more modern dress, it never did so, preferring on each occasion to rebuild in styles ten or fifteen years out of date. In part this was due to the generally conservative architects and contractors who designed the replacements. But as Thomas suggests, ultimate praise or blame devolves to their employers, the Philadelphia businessmen who effectively controlled the town's destiny. Far from desiring a summer resort that was up-to-date and tourist-prone, they preferred to keep *their* Cape May quaint and quiet. Perhaps they had all been reading *The Horticulturist.*

• • • • •

"You know," wrote James Fennimore Cooper, "that no American who is at all comfortable in life will share his dwelling with another."

Perhaps not, but it is apparent that he was often willing to share party walls with strangers. For reasons that are not altogether fathomable, attached housing has had a long history in the United States. With an entire continent yawning empty before them, the Jamestown colonists chose to construct some of their earliest dwellings as rowhouses. Semi-communal buildings of this sort were built only spottily during the 1700s, but by the middle of the nineteenth century, they were an established fact of life in most eastern cities.

In the twentieth century it has become almost a reflex to think of rowhouses as squalid tenements, the last resort of the working poor if not the totally indigent. This makes it difficult for most of us to realize that in the late nineteenth century, single-family rowhouses were virtual mansions for the middle class. A comfortable brownstone in New York City rose four full stories over a raised basement and had room aplenty for a large family and a servant or two as well. Smaller rowhouses, which could be as narrow as twelve feet across the front, offered less space and fewer amenities but were still spacious by comparison with the average apartment today. At their best, rowhouses were roomy, airy, well-lighted, had the latest in conveniences, and were located near the center of town. Unfortunately most of them have long since been replaced by or divided into multiple-family tenements.

In larger towns the advent of attached houses could usually be justified by the pressing need for groundspace. But the fact that rowhouses were also common in smaller towns where space was abundant suggests that many of them were erected not out of necessity so much as simple greed on the part of landlords and developers. In any case, rowhouse building had become an inveterate habit on the East Coast by the end of the century, and examples from the period can still be found even in tiny New England towns surrounded by wilderness.

Because of the danger of fire, most municipalities outlawed frame construction in attached housing by the 1850s or thereabouts. From then on, the urban landscape came to be dominated by brick rowhouses. In New York City, however, most of the raw brick was sooner or later covered with a veneer of brownstone, a readily available and relatively inexpensive material. When it became fashionable as well in the late 1840s, the combination proved unbeatable, with the result—as Edith Wharton put it in *The Age of Innocence*— that brownstone soon "coated New York like a cold chocolate sauce."

In terms of style, Victorian rowhouses followed the same general evolution from Gothic to Queen Anne that was then taking place in the country and suburbs. In the city, however, stylistic changes were marked more by ornamental than structural differences. Designed for narrow city lots, row and town houses maintained the same tall, thin proportions and three-fold facade arrangements throughout the century. For the most part it was only the decorative details that distinguished one rowhouse style from another.

The exigencies of urban life naturally tended to favor some architectural styles over others. Those that did not lend themselves readily to the constraints of narrow lots and standardized rowhouse formats usually received short shrift in the city. The Gothic Revival style, for instance, was never a popular one for rowhouses, partly because it was firmly identified with country living and partly because its sweeping gables and irregular massing made it problematic in an urban context. For similar reasons the later picturesque styles never fared well in town. Attached houses in the Queen Anne mode are rare, and urban

approximations of the suburban Stick style virtually unknown. Still, some interesting attempts to bend these unpromising styles to the demands of rowhouses can be found here and there.

The Italianate and Second Empire styles which were more adaptable, did better in the city. The former began to supplant Greek Revival rowhouses in the late 1840s, and the latter came into vogue after the Civil War. However, aside from the mansard roofs that distinguish Second Empire examples, the differences between the two styles were slight: their ornamental features— sills, lintels, and cornice brackets—were virtually identical.

The strange fondness for rowhouses that characterized the East Coast is just one of a number of differences that set the region's architecture apart from the rest of America. Although the Victorian house had made its debut on the Eastern Seaboard, its example was not copied exactly elsewhere in the country, and some of the differences are worth noting.

For starters, East Coast Victorians tended to be more conservative—or, if one prefers, tasteful—than their counterparts in the West. In the East the most dubious taste was more often expressed in terms of scale and sheer opulence—as in some of the Vanderbilt mansions—than in outlandish shapes and ornament. To someone accustomed to the farfetched vulgarity of select Victorian survivors in, for instance, Texas and California, the architecture of the East, despite a few gaudy exceptions, seems generally staid and restrained.

Several explanations for this suggest themselves. One is what might be called the momentum of decorum. With so many prim colonial houses on the scene to serve as models, eastern architects, builders, and owners may well have been inhibited from experimenting too freely when designing and constructing a new house. It was far easier for a California lumber baron or a Texas cattleman to risk bad taste than it was for a Hartford banker. And even if architects and builders ignored the silent rebuke of the older houses in the region—and there are historic photographs to show that many of them did— later generations were quick to undo the sins of their fathers. In the East, the most outrageous expressions of the age were often modified, colonialized, and painted a seemly and decorous white by subsequent owners.

Another difference that separates East Coast architecture from that of the rest of the country is its choice of building materials. To the eternal surprise of Europeans, the vast majority of American houses are of wood-frame construction. In this, eastern houses are no exception; but the percentage of brick and stone dwellings in the region is distinctly higher than elsewhere in the country. This was probably a reflection of the European bias for masonry. But the voice of Andrew Jackson Downing can also be heard in the choir.

Although he acknowledged, somewhat resignedly, that wooden houses had to be accorded at least provisional sanction in the United States, his material preferences were made crystal clear in *The Architecture of Country Houses* when he wrote: "We greatly prefer a cottage of brick or rough stone, to one of wood."

The eastern bias for masonry may have been most evident in the upscale mansions of the wealthy, but it was apparent also in smaller homes. Some of them were *actually* constructed of brick or stone, but a great many more only seemed to be. For all the talk of truth to materials, the ideal was not always upheld in nineteenth-century building. Modest frame houses were often covered with rusticated wooden siding or smooth-matched flushboard to simulate stone or stucco. Even *Lyndhurst*, Alexander Jackson Davis' finest Gothic castle, contains wooden details painted to resemble stone.

Still, unabashed frame construction was endemic in American building, so it should not be much of a surprise to learn that it, too, had its advocates. Quite a number of the architects of the day had, after all, begun their careers as carpenters. Henry Austin, George F. Barber, Stephen Decatur Button, Isaac Hobbs, George Palliser, and Samuel Sloan were just a few of them; and it is worth noting that all continued to design frame buildings throughout their careers.

Another architect, Gervase Wheeler, went so far as to suggest that frame dwellings in America constituted "a style of erection which may be considered as almost national." As quoted in the *Architecture of Country Houses*, he went on to deplore the fact that they were often disguised to look as though they were built of brick or stone. "Attempts to imitate in wood, effects that can only legitimately be produced in stone or other material, may for a time please the vulgar eye, but they cannot ultimately fail to be as unsparingly condemned as they deserve."

Given his enthusiasm for frame construction, it is not surprising that Wheeler was one of the first architects in the East to express an interest in the balloon frame that had recently blossomed in the Midwest. His *Homes for the People* (1855) contains one of the first published accounts—albeit an incomplete one—of the framing system that had such far-reaching effects on house design in the late Victorian era.

Owing, once again, to the weight of tradition, it took twenty years or so for eastern architects and builders to adopt the new system wholeheartedly. The heavy timber frame, after all, had been on the continent more than two hundred years when the balloon frame first appeared. The partial description offered by Wheeler followed the practical introduction of the new technique by less than a decade; but it was another ten years before George Woodward published the first complete technical explanation of the process in his *Country Homes* (1865). And it seems not to have been in common use on the Eastern Seaboard before the late 1860s. Even Richard Morris Hunt's Griswold House (1863), which has been linked to the balloon frame because of its stick-style surface decoration, was actually constructed on the older post-and-beam system.

• • • • •

The tradition of wooden building that had begun with the board-and-batten cottages of the Gothic Revival culminated in the Queen Anne and Shingle styles of the late Victorian era. Of the two, the former achieved broad success, but the latter never became truly popular. Individual in design, expensive to construct, and closely identified with exclusive New England seaside resorts, the houses of the Shingle style were not conceived to appeal to a broad spectrum of home builders in America—though they did help start a fad for shingled wall surfaces in the late 1880s. On the other hand, the style appealed immensely to architects and historians who saw in its contoured lines and organic planning vital links between the colonial past and the modernist future.

However, the essential character of American building is not to be found in the designs of high-style architects like Richard Morris Hunt and Henry Hobson Richardson, nor yet in the scattered masterpieces of the vernacular tradition. For better or worse, it is to be found in the prodigious outpourings of the low-art practitioners—Barber, Button, Hobbs, Palliser, and a host of unsung others. At about the same time that the vaunted Shingle style was rising in such millionaires' haunts as Newport and Tuxedo Park, the Queen Anne style was conquering the rest of the country. Taking the form of expansive country villas and abbreviated suburban houses, it became one of the favorites of the middle class and by century's end could be found in small towns and suburbs in every corner of the United States.

Not surprisingly, most of the high-style, European-trained architects working in the Northeast abandoned the simple traditions of the wooden building as soon as they could attract a clientele willing to pay for limestone and marble. Although Hunt had adumbrated the Stick style in his famous Griswold House in Newport, and Richardson had arrived at what many consider to be the prototypical Queen Anne in his Watts-Sherman House in the same town, both went on to build the most baronial of stone mansions for their wealthiest clients. The same can be said of McKim, Mead, and White who, along with Richardson had created the Shingle style.

From the Civil War until the end of the century, the United States experienced an economic growth to which previous history offers no parallel.

The advent of railroads and heavy industry was accompanied by a vehement and unfettered capitalism beholden to no law save that of supply and demand, a piece of legislation which it often manipulated to suit its own ends. It took the country the better part of a half century to learn that uncontrolled competition generally issues in monopoly. In the meantime some enormous personal fortunes were accumulated and some amazing pieces of architecture built.

These included several huge mansions which were commissioned by the heirs of Commodore Vanderbilt in the last two decades of the century. In his own, more egalitarian age, A.J. Downing had warned against building just such houses as these with arguments that were half moral, half practical. On the one hand, anticipating Veblen, he implied that it was not quite fitting for wealth to express itself so illiberally in a republic. But, more pragmatically, he also argued that attempts to establish great European-style estates in this country were doomed to failure. Noting that the United States lacked the laws of primogeniture and entail that effectively ensured the transmission of intact inheritances in England, he confidently predicted that such estates would ultimately be broken up by a pack of squabbling heirs, no one of whom could afford to maintain the whole.

This line of reasoning may have been plausible in the 1850s, but it seemed to fall apart a few decades later when it had to contend with the enormous fortunes of the Gilded Age. By hook or crook—often the latter—Commodore Vanderbilt had managed to acquire more than 100 million dollars during his earthly career. And in the space of a single decade, his son, William Henry, more or less doubled that amount. When the accumulated wealth passed to a third generation of Vanderbilts, it set off a spate of building the like of which had never been seen before on this side of the Atlantic.

To the delight of European art dealers, Indiana quarrymen, Italian stonemasons, and a few privileged architects, the Commodore's grandsons started a fad for costly mansions that was quickly taken up by other members of the New York-Newport set. The Beaux-Arts palaces that resulted set new standards for lavish building in America. Even some Europeans were impressed.

The scale and expense of these town houses and summer villas seemed to embody a complete rejection of the ideals of the early Victorian period— the triumph of wealth and academic classicism over the egalitarian values and simple designs that Downing and others had stressed. But, as Alan Gowans has noted, Richard Morris Hunt's last two projects, *Biltmore* in Asheville, North Carolina, and *The Breakers* in Newport, are nothing less than refined recapitulations—albeit on an enormous scale—of the two earliest Victorian styles, the Gothic and the Italianate. In addition, these two enormous limestone palaces are notable as examples of prophecy fulfilled. Both have long since been abandoned by those who inherited them and are now open to the general public as house museums. A.J. Downing, it seems, may have had the last word after all.

KINGSCOTE

1841: Newport, Rhode Island

Founded in 1639 by religious dissidents from Massachusetts, Newport soon became one of the most important ports on the East Coast. In the seventeenth and eighteenth centuries it prospered playing host to traders, smugglers, even a few pirates. And its streets were literally paved with profits from the slave trade.

Just before the Revolutionary War, the town accounted for more foreign commerce than New York City. But its early importance came to an end in 1776 when it was occupied and half destroyed by the British. After Independence it never recovered its former momentum as a seafaring town.

In the last half of the nineteenth century, however, Newport emerged as the most elegant and exclusive summer resort in America—the playground of the Victorian rich and famous. In the Gilded Age, which began after the Civil War, it became the seasonal nesting ground of millionaires—Astors, Vanderbilts, and Goelets—who flocked north in droves from Fifth Avenue each summer.

All this was just in its beginnings when the house shown here was being built in the late 1830s. Newport had only recently been discovered as a summer colony, and visitors were just starting to erect vacation cottages of their own.

Kingscote, as it was named by a subsequent owner, was originally the summer home of George Noble Jones, a wealthy Savannah resident who attended Newport religiously until the outbreak of the Civil War. Apparently fearing the place might be confiscated in the wake of Fort Sumpter, he deeded it to a Canadian relative and headed back to Dixie.

The house was designed by Richard Upjohn (1802-78), an English cabinetmaker who went on to become the most distinguished architect of Gothic Revival churches in America. *Kingscote* was one of the earliest houses in Newport—or the rest of the country for that matter—to adopt the picturesque aesthetic that had recently made its way across the Atlantic from England. By comparison with the rectangular boxes of the earlier Georgian and Federal styles it was highly irregular in plan and elevation, with wings and bay windows leaping out of the main block of the house and gables and dormers interrupting the roof line.

The details, too, were picturesque and highly ornamental. High-flying chimney pots, undulating bargeboards, diamond-paned windows, Gothic label molds, a hint of battlements over the front bay—all these announced that architecture in America was about to enter a romantic phase. And the colors were also new. In keeping with the doctrine that a house should blend with its surroundings, *Kingscote* was painted somber, picturesque gray instead of blinding, classical white.

In 1864 the house was acquired by William H. King, brother of Edward King who owned another Upjohn creation (p. 53). In the 1880s it was enlarged by the firm of McKim, Mead, and White, exponents of the Shingle style, who contributed the turreted addition at the rear of the house. Today *Kingscote* is maintained by the Preservation Society of Newport County and is open for public tours.

LYNDHURST
1838-65: Tarrytown, New York

Among the manifestations of the Gothic Revival in America were dwellings that frankly imitated castles. Notable examples began to arise in New York and Virginia in the late 1830s, and they continued to appear in new stylistic guises until the end of the century. They were inspired in part by the medieval relics that dotted Britain and the Continent, but much of their romantic appeal derived from the fantasies of Sir Walter Scott and other popular novelists.

Even A.J. Downing, who suggested that such houses were not quite appropriate for a republic, fell under their spell. His own home in Newburgh was noticeably castle-like, and of *Lyndhurst*, designed by Alexander Jackson Davis, he was enthusiastic. "I think it does you great credit—" he wrote the architect, "indeed I have never seen anything to equal it. . . ."

The house was the first of several substantial villas that Davis designed to grace the banks of the Hudson. Originally built as the summer retreat of General William Paulding, a wealthy lawyer and New York City politician, the castle was diminutive by European standards. But in the 1860s, when its second owner, George W. Merritt, hired Davis to design some additions, the house nearly doubled in size. After it had grown to something approaching true baronial proportions it was acquired by a baron of *sorts*, the egregious Jay Gould.

Not all contemporary opinion on the house was as favorable as Downing's. The breezy diarist Phillip Hone dismissed it as "an immense edifice with no room in it," and predicted that it would one day be known as "Paulding's folly." But today *Lyndhurst* is generally considered the finest Gothic Revival castle on this side of the Atlantic. It displays almost all of the details characteristic of the style: pinnacled towers, castellated parapets, tudor and lancet arches, to name a few.

Its basic construction material is brick sheathed with Ossining marble— quarried, they say, by convicts from nearby Sing Sing prison. The porch supports and some other details, however, are of wood.

Set on a knoll overlooking a broad stretch of the Hudson known as the Tappan Zee and surrounded by sixty-three acres of formal gardens and picturesque landscaping, the house has been declared a National Historic Landmark. Since 1961 it has been a property of the National Trust for Historic Preservation which has made it available for public tours.

Figure 1: from Downing's *Treatise on the Theory and Practice of Landscape Gardening.*

DELAMATER HOUSE
1844: Rhinebeck, New York

Besides castles like *Lyndhurst* (p. 13), Alexander Jackson Davis also designed cottages. His earliest residential work dates from the years when he was in partnership with Ithiel Town and includes examples in the Greek Revival mode; but he soon began to champion the Gothic as the best and most fitting style for rural houses in America. Partly because they were prominently featured in A.J. Downing's several books, Davis' cottage designs were enormously influential and helped create the Gothic fever that swept much of the country in the 1840s and '50s.

Because his spreading fame coincided with improved service and reduced postage rates, Davis was one of the first architects in the country who was able to make efficient use of the mails to conduct business. Though he doesn't seem to have advertised formally, it is clear that he received numerous letters requesting his services. If a client could pay his fee, Davis was happy to travel wherever necessary to do a job. But if something less expensive was in order, he was also happy to stay home and dispatch working drawings through the mails. By the late 1840s he was using this method to service customers as far away as Virginia and the Midwest.

The house pictured here was closer to home, but the principle was the same. For a mere twenty-five dollars, Henry Delamater, a well-to-do Rhinebeck merchant, ordered plans from the architect's office in New York and let local carpenters do the rest.

Though it seems Davis never made an appearance at the construction site, the house that resulted is a particularly fine example of his work. Like the Brooks House in Salem (p. 25) it is similar to a design for "A Cottage in the English or Rural Gothic Style" that was included in Downing's *Cottage Residences* (1842). Unlike the Massachusetts example, however, the Delamater house makes no pretensions about its underlying structure: the board-and-batten siding is frank in revealing that it is of wood-frame construction.

Several other features associated with the Gothic Revival can also be seen here: steep-pitched center gables with decorative bargeboards and pinnacles; a pointed window hood; diamond-paned glass; diagonally-placed chimney pots; and—on the porch—Tudor arches and posts decorated with lacy openwork. The present color scheme, incidentally, is believed to be faithful to the original.

In perfect repair, Henry Delamater's former residence serves today as the guest house of a local hotel and is open for group tours by appointment.

Figure 2: from *Cottage Residences*.

BOWEN HOUSE,
ROSELAND COTTAGE
1846: Woodstock, Connecticut

Roseland Cottage was the country retreat of Henry Bowen (1813-1896), a native of Woodstock who made his fortune in New York City but never severed the ties that bound him to his home town. A sixth-generation descendant of one of the village founders, he was educated at local academies and worked for a few years in his father's store and tavern before leaving home. In New York he soon established himself as a partner in a silk import business and also became the publisher of two newspapers, *The Brooklyn Union* and *The Independent*, the latter a Congregationalist journal with a strong anti-slavery stance.

Attacked in print because his firm refused to endorse the Fugitive Slave Law passed as part of The Compromise of 1850, Bowen responded with a broadside that insisted on freedom of expression and a clear-cut division between commerce and ideas. "We wish it distinctly understood," it said, "that our goods, and not our principles are on the market."

In 1846 he constructed the cottage which served as his country seat for the remainder of his years. Called *Roseland* for the gardens that surround it, the house is a particularly fine version of the Gothic Cottage *ornee* that Downing and others thought singularly appropriate for the country home of a gentleman. The function of such a house was symbolic and aesthetic as well as practical. Besides providing all the comforts of home away from home it was also an emblem of genteel rusticity, a sort of stage set that affirmed the simple virtues of life in the country.

The construction was performed by Edwin Eaton, a house carpenter from Chapin, Connecticut, but its design is credited to Joseph Collins Wells, an English architect who had come to the United States to build Gothic Revival churches. He was the architect of Brooklyn's Plymouth Church of the Pilgrims, which Bowen helped found for the flamboyant minister Henry Ward Beecher a few years after *Roseland Cottage* was completed. Wells' nationality may explain the large scale and extended plan of the house as well as its multiplicity of gables—all of these were more typical of English than of American cottages. Its wealth of Gothic details includes board-and-batten siding, steep-pitched gables, serpentine bargeboards, diamond-paned windows, porch supports with wooden openwork, pointed window hoods, and picturesque chimney pots. The house is also noteworthy in having two distinct fronts, one functional, one presentational.

In the ninety years since Henry Bowen's death, *Roseland Cottage* has been carefully maintained—first by his heirs and more recently by the Society for the Preservation of New England Antiquities. It was acquired by the Society in 1970 and is now listed on the National Register of Historic Places. Adorned with fittings and furnishings dating from the 1840s to the 1880s, it is open for public tours each year from mid-May to mid-September.

WILLIAM J. ROTCH HOUSE

1846: New Bedford, Massachusetts

William J. Rotch (1819-1893) was the heir apparent of a Quaker whaling family that had been active in Massachusetts for more than a century when he was born. His ancestors—a bewildering succession of Williams and Josephs—had dominated New Bedford ever since they arrived from Nantucket in 1765.

Rotch grew up just as the famous whaling port was making a transition from maritime pursuits to textile manufacture. As everyone expected, he graduated from Harvard in 1838, but he may have surprised some of the townsfolk when he was elected mayor at age thirty-three. He also founded a mill, took a seat in the state legislature, and served for more than forty years as president of the Friends Academy. In his later years he was a man of means and influence and held interests in most of the important businesses in town.

When the house shown here was constructed, however, he was still in his twenties. As the story goes, Rotch and his bride, Emily Morgan, honeymooned on the Hudson where they were much impressed with the Gothic Revival cottages that were springing up on its banks. A few years later they startled New Bedford with a similarly inspired cottage of their own. Rotch's father is said to have been most displeased with it, but it is now regarded as one of the most distinguished of Alexander Jackson Davis' Gothic cottages.

The design traces to a sumptuous rendering that Davis had prepared, probably as a speculative plan, in 1838. In April of 1845 Rotch wrote to Davis requesting his services, and by the end of May he had working drawings in hand. The construction was carried out by Augustus A. Greene & Company, local carpenters who were delighted and impressed with Davis' plans but—according to Rotch—a little intimidated by the elaborate carving required by some of the details. In the end, at least part of this work was ordered from a New York craftsman named John Gallier.

Some years after the house was completed, Davis' original drawing was reproduced as a woodcut: first in an 1849 issue of *The Horticulturist*, A.J. Downing's "Journal of Rural Taste," and later in his *Architecture of Country Houses* (1852). Except that it doesn't show the small dormers that flank the central gable, the drawing mirrors the completed house in all essentials.

In commenting on the design, Downing recommended brick as the material of choice. But, in fact, Rotch built the house in wood, though he covered it with horizontal shiplap painted to resemble stucco. Downing also notes that the house cost six thousand dollars to build. Presumably this included the architect's very reasonable fee—$150 for working drawings, specifications and his visit to New Bedford. As for the lot, Rotch purchased it from his grandfather "for one dollar and love and goodwill."

"Altogether," Downing wrote, "we should say that the character expressed by the exterior of this design is that of a man or family of domestic tastes, but with strong aspirations after something higher than social pleasures." Today the house is the home of the current mayor of New Bedford.

Figure 3: "Cottage Villa in the Rural Gothic Style," from *The Architecture of Country Houses*.

HENRY TEN EYCK HOUSE

c. 1847: Cazenovia, New York

The village of Cazenovia, southeast of Syracuse, was founded in 1793 by John Linclaen, an agent for the Holland Land Company. The town, which he named for his boss, Theophile Casanove, was laid out on part of the 64,000 acres he had purchased along the proposed route of the Western Turnpike. Because this was the preferred road for New Englanders stricken with Ohio fever, the new settlement prospered as a stopping place for travelers and drovers in the first quarter of the nineteenth century. With the opening of the Erie Canal in 1825, however, overland traffic began to decline, and land prices in the village fell.

Strangely, this worked to the detriment of the Indians who still inhabited the area. In *Upstate: Records and Recollection of Northern New York*, Edmund Wilson records that "The Oneidas in 1842 were mostly induced under false pretenses to remove to Green Bay, Wisconsin; and such of the nation as remained were driven off their land on the pretext of a mortgage being foreclosed." This hindrance to progress eliminated, Cazenovia developed as a quiet but popular summer community—a character it has never entirely lost.

Among the town's surviving nineteenth-century structures is this cottage in the Gothic Revival style. It was built in the late 1840s by a merchant and entrepreneur named Jacob Ten Eyck for his son Henry. No records have survived to show who designed and built it, but with its pointed gables, bargeboards, and board-and-batten siding, it is clearly related to the Dowingesque cottages that were rising on the Hudson at about the same time.

The house served as a residence until 1965 when it was put up for sale and rumors began circulating that it might be razed to make way for a parking lot. Alarmed preservationists contacted a local benefactor who agreed to purchase the cottage provided a valid use could be found for it. It was subsequently pressed into service as a town office building and eventually became the focus of a restoration project, spearheaded by the Cazenovia Preservation Foundation, in which virtually every civic group in the village took part. Under the supervision of preservation architect Carl Stearns, the original woodwork and other details were carefully duplicated, and the house was completely restored by the early 1980s. *The Gothic Cottage*, as it is now officially known, is listed on the National Register and is open to the public.

JUSTIN SMITH MORRILL HOUSE
1851: Strafford, Vermont

An especially fine example of American Carpenter's Gothic, this house was once the home of a Yankee storekeeper turned U.S. senator. Justin Smith Morrill (1810-1898) was born the son of a farmer and part-time blacksmith in the tiny village of Strafford. By his twenties he had established himself as a partner in the village store and by the age of thirty-eight had prospered so nicely that he retired to what he thought would be a life of books and genteel farming. Instead he was elected to Congress, where he served in the House from 1854 until he became a senator in 1866.

In all he spent forty-five years on Capitol Hill and by all accounts was a respected and admired member of the legislature. The most important bill he sponsored was the Land Grant College Act of 1862 which made public lands available to states that wished to establish colleges "for the benefit of the agricultural and technical arts."

Throughout his political career the house in Strafford served as Morrill's Vermont residence. Completed in 1851 and laid out with landscaped gardens in the best tradition of A.J. Downing, it reflected the Gothic influence that had spread from the Hudson to New England.

The house was built on a braced-frame system, a precursor of the balloon frame that dominated wooden-house construction later in the nineteenth century. The flushboard siding is made up of thin strips of clear pine. It was originally stained dark umber but was later painted a delicate rose in imitation of pink sandstone. The "embattled" bay window at the front of the house and the enclosed porch with its castellated roof, slender turret, and window tracery are unusually castle-like for a rural cottage. These details were added to the basic structure about 1860.

According to local tradition, Morrill designed the house himself, but other evidence suggests that it may have been based on a standardized plan. Measured drawings prepared by the Historic American Buildings Survey show that the General Manuel Vallejo House—one of a trio of identical, prefabricated cottages that were shipped from New England to California during the gold rush era—is strikingly similar to the Morrill cottage both in plan and in some of its details.

Today the house and grounds are maintained by the State of Vermont as the Justin Smith Morrill Homestead. Furnished with family possessions and other memorabilia, the cottage is open to the public during the summer months.

Figure 4: from HAB Survey drawings of the General Vallejo House, Sonoma, California.

HENRY MASON BROOKS HOUSE

1851: Salem, Massachusetts

If the Rotch House (p. 19) is guilty of mild dissimulation in attempting to look like a stucco-covered cottage, the Brooks House is positively mendacious. Though it purports to be of stone, it is actually a frame house covered with flat wooden panels sawn and chamfered to resemble smooth-cut masonry blocks.

Such transparent duplicity was never meant to fool anyone, of course, but the gesture itself indicates that the Old-World ideal of masonry construction was alive and well in nineteenth-century America.

Like the residence that Henry Delamater built in Rhinebeck, New York (p. 15), the Brooks house is clearly based on a design for "A Cottage in the English or Rural Gothic Style," which appeared in A.J. Downing's *Cottage Residences* (fig. 2). It seems to have been the result of a typical collaboration between Downing and Alexander Jackson Davis, the former contributing ideas and rough sketches, the latter supplying details and finished drawings. Of the design, Downing makes special mention of the porch—which he considered essential for hot American summers—and notes the pains taken to break up its horizontal lines in order to make it more consistent with Gothic verticality.

No details about who constructed the house are available, but it is recorded that it was built for Timothy Brooks of Salem. Just a few years after it was completed, however, Brooks died, and it passed to his son, Henry Mason, who resided there all his life.

Though the Gothic Revival style had passed out of fashion by the time he died in 1898, this cottage must have made a perfect residence for the younger Brooks, an antiquarian both by temperament and avocation. According to a memoir published by Salem's Essex Institute, "He enjoyed a newspaper that was one hundred years old far better than one that was fresh from the press."

As secretary of the Institute from 1888 to 1898, Brooks urged his fellow members to save everything and to throw nothing away. And he seems to have practiced what he preached, collecting books and newspapers, stamps and coins, chantey songs, profane jokes, and quotations of all sorts. "He had," his memoirist tells us, "the amazing faculty of recalling the dates not only of every important event but also of every unimportant one." He was also a gifted mimic and could do an uncanny portrayal of Ralph Waldo Emerson, "so perfect indeed that the distinguished speaker seemed to stand before us." In addition he was an excellent calligrapher and might have made a good forger, for he could duplicate all of the signatures on the Declaration of Independence from memory, and he sometimes amused himself by endorsing greenbacks in George Washington's hand.

Brooks was aware that his own passions might seem eccentric to outsiders and tried to remind them that antiquarianism also had a practical side. He had a precocious understanding of the value of historic preservation to the local economy and rightly predicted that Salem's past would one day be an important resource. In the meantime, he did what he could to preserve it.

That he was remembered by his eulogist as "genial," might have amused him; for he had noticed that in the newspapers every bride was either "agreeable" or "genteel" and that the dead were always "virtuous" or, at the very least, "amiable."

GREEN-MELDRIM HOUSE
c. 1850s: Savannah, Georgia

After cutting a fiery swath through Georgia in the fall of 1864, General William Tecumseh Sherman entered the undefended city of Savannah on December 22. Three days later, in a letter home, he described the quarters that had been placed at his disposal. "I am at this moment in an elegant chamber of the house of a gentleman named Green. This house is elegant and splendidly furnished with pictures and statuary. My bedroom has a bath and dressing room attached which look out of proportion to my poor baggage."

Sherman used the house as his headquarters for a little over a month while gathering his forces for a march on Charleston. During this interlude he was the guest of Charles Green (1807-1881), an English cotton merchant and shipper who had made Savannah his home some years before. Green's hospitality may have been motivated by a desire to spare his adopted city the fate that had been meted out to Atlanta. But he may also have been genuinely relieved to see the arrival of the Union troops: the naval blockade that had isolated the city for most of the war had not been good for business.

Green had built his lavish residence in better times. Although city records indicate that it was constructed about 1861, Green family documents suggest that it may date from as early as 1853. In any case, when it was new, the house was generally considered one of the finest homes in Savannah. William Howard Russell, Civil War correspondent for the *London Times*, went so far as to compare it with the mansions of New York's Fifth Avenue. Much of its splendor, however, is hidden within. Most of the construction budget was expended on the elegant interior appointments that so impressed General Sherman. Of the $93,000 Green spent, about half went for flagstones, laths, lime, planks, bricks, and books, all of which were imported from England.

The design, by the New York architect John S. Norris is unusual in combining Gothic details with a flat-roofed, essentially rectangular structure. Gothic features include the battlements at the roofline and above the oriels and the rectangular drip molds over the upper windows. The fine cast-iron work also displays a variety of Tudor and other motifs associated with the "pointed" style. Except for the ornamental chimney stacks, however, there is little suggestion of the picturesque extensions—gables, towers, pinnacles—that generally mark Gothic houses.

In 1892 the mansion was acquired by Peter W. Meldrim, a prominent Georgia jurist who served a term as president of the American Bar Association, and it remained in his family until 1943. Today it serves as the Parish House of St. John's Episcopal Church of Savannah. It has been designated a National Historic Landmark and is open to the public for tours by appointment.

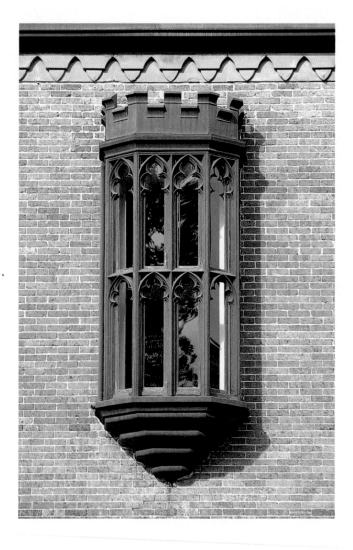

THE WEDDING CAKE HOUSE
1826-56: Kennebunk, Maine

Originally built during the Federal period, *The Wedding Cake House* was later remodeled to reflect the Gothic Revival style that attained currency in the mid-1850s. The house seems to have acquired its name as the result of a story that some inventive local concocted to satisfy persistent tourist questions about how such a fanciful dwelling came into being.

As one version has it, a ship's captain is called away on his wedding day by an emergency at sea. When he returns—weeks, months, even years later—he rewards his bride for her patience by building their lovenest in the form of a wedding cake. In some tellings, he even whittles the gingerbread while making sail for home.

As it happens, however, the house was actually the work of George Washington Bourne (1801-1856), a fourth-generation shipbuilder whose family had been active on the Maine coast since the early 1700s. After constructing thirty-three wooden sailing vessels in something less than twenty years, he retired in 1853 and turned his attention to remodeling the house he had built for his bride twenty-five years previously.

When an outbuilding behind the main house burned to the ground, Bourne replaced it with a new frame building which he covered with vertical boards and battens and decorated with a wealth of Gothic details—pointed arches, castellations, false buttresses, and crocketed pinnacles. This completed, he hired a young ships carpenter, Thomas Durrell, as an assistant and set to work on the house itself. When the job was finished, the brick structure was encased in an airy wooden exoskeleton composed of six elaborately carved but utterly nonfunctional buttresses linked together with pointed arches and lacy spandrels.

The result was decidedly Gothic, but Gothic of a sort that had more to do with ecclesiastical models than any of the cottages Downing and Davis might have advocated. Evidence suggests, in fact, that *The Wedding Cake House* was inspired by nothing less than the enormous Cathedral of Milan in Italy. According to family members, numerous sketches of the famous church were found among Bourne's papers after his death. And the two structures do share undeniable, if superficial, similarities.

Whatever its source, the house is a unique and idiosyncratic example of American Carpenter's Gothic. Thanks to a new owner, Mary Burnett, who restored and refurbished it as a private residence in the 1970s, it continues to amaze and perplex tourists and architectural historians alike.

SHURTLEFF HOUSE

c. 1850: Winslow, Maine

Although no certain information about who designed and built this house is available, it is assumed to be the work of its original owner, Jonas B. Shurtleff (1805-1863). A New Englander by birth and upbringing, Shurtleff had spent most of his adult life in Pennsylvania where he published a newspaper, *The Tioga Country Patriot*. In 1847 he relocated to Waterville, Maine, where he ran a bookstore for two years before purchasing property near the small town of Winslow. He is thought to have built the house between 1850 and 1853.

Essentially square in plan, it is a two-story frame structure with a broad, cross-gabled roof. It might be a typical example of vernacular house building, except for some decorative touches that indicate some knowledge of current architectural styles. The side and transom lights surrounding the doorway, for instance, may be survivals from the Greek Revival period, and the three-part window above the portico seems to be a rural builders' attempt at a Palladian arch.

Most of the other flourishes, however, are Gothic in inspiration. The squared-off drip molds above the windows, the board-and-batten siding, the steep gables with their bargeboards and pinnacles—all are part of the vocabulary of forms that, thanks to Downing and others, were available to vernacular builders by midcentury.

ETHRIDGE HOUSE
1853: Sparta, Georgia

Though it enjoyed its greatest popularity in the Northeast, the Gothic Cottage style was by no means unknown in the South. Like the Shurtleff House in Winslow, Maine (p. 31), this example in Georgia seems to be a vernacular approximation of Gothic styling. Its steep gables, bargeboards, and board-and-batten siding would have been at home anywhere north of the Mason-Dixon Line. But it also displays some regional twists.

The cusps of the bargeboards, for instance, are tipped with stylized acorns—a persistant motif in southern decorative schemes. And the house itself is set on brick piers—a regional building practice which promoted cooling and ventilation. The most distinctly southern accent, however, is found in the broad veranda with its airy, cookie-cutter patterning and stylized floral applique.

The area around Sparta suffered a good deal of damage during Sherman's March, but the Ethridge House survived unscathed. Perhaps it reminded the Yankees of home.

JAMES SLEDGE HOUSE

c. 1860: Athens, Georgia

Athens, the largest city in the piedmont country of northeastern Georgia, is most often remembered for its Greek Revival, antebellum homes; but it also has a number of structures from the Victorian era, including Italianate, Second Empire, and Queen Anne houses. In addition—as the example shown here demonstrates—at least one representative of the Gothic Revival style has managed to survive in town.

Built just before the Civil War, the house bears the name of its first owner, James Sledge. During the conflict he was the editor of an Athens newspaper called *The Southern Banner*, the politics of which can be surmised from its title. Bankrupt after Appomattox, Sledge lost the house to foreclosure, and it was soon acquired by one Ferdinand Phinizy, who had sold him the lot a few years before.

Phinizy (1819-1889) was a wealthy merchant, landowner, and money lender who had the same name as his grandfather, an Italian orphan who had arrived in Georgia along with French troops dispatched to bolster the American Revolution in the late 1770s. From these unlikely beginnings he went on to become one of the richest merchants in the state.

The younger Phinizy, it seems, also had a talent for business. Before the Civil War he acquired a fortune in land, cotton, and slaves, and during the fighting he sold Confederate bonds and helped run cotton through the blockades. Just like Rhett Butler. When the shooting was over his fortune was in ruins, but he quickly rebuilt it with new investments in real estate, railroads, and insurance.

Phinizy is known to have financed a number of speculative houses in Athens, and it is conjectured that he built this one as well. Though evidently inspired by similar sources, the house is rather different form the run of Gothic Revival cottages that were popular in the North a decade earlier. The steep-pitched gables that dominate the facade are obviously Gothic, but the stuccoed brick and cast-iron porch work lend the house a distinct regional flavor. Iron work of the sort seen here was a feature of many southern houses from the Greek Revival period onward. The eagles' heads and entwined garland motifs in this example are especially fine and are thought to have been produced locally.

The Sledge House, which now serves as the residence of the grandson of the second Ferdinand Phinizy, is located in the Cobbham section of Athens. The area was subdivided in the 1830s by John A. Cobb, a farmer who had extensive landholdings on the outskirts of town. In the nineteenth century it became one of the city's premier residential districts, and—despite twentieth-century encroachment—it has managed to retain much of its original character. In recent decades the neighborhood has been designated as a National Register District.

Dr. A.B. NOBLES HOUSE

c. 1865: Tarboro vicinity, North Carolina

Unusual both for its brick construction and as a rare example of Gothic Revival architecture in North Carolina, this house was originally the home of Dr. Allen B. Nobles. Nobles was born in North Carolina in 1823, but studied medicine in Cincinnati. He practiced as a physician up until—and presumably during—the Civil War, but at the end of the conflict he settled down near Tarboro and devoted himself to progressive farming.

His house is said to have been constructed between 1865 and 1870, and is thought to be the work of a local builder, Thomas Coates, who is known to have erected a similar dwelling within the Tarboro city limits. Whoever the builder was, he made skillful use of brickwork to create the corbelled bays and Tudor-arched windows. The design, which may have been derived from a pattern book, is a variation on the same cross-gabled, L-shaped combination seen in the Justin Smith Morrill House (p. 23). The Nobles House is also noteworthy for underscoring, once again, the relationship between scientific farming and Gothic Revival cottage architecture. The connection, no doubt, traces to A.J. Downing's influential magazine *The Horticulturist*, which simultaneously promulgated a taste for Gothic cottages and encouraged the adoption of improved agricultural methods.

GOTHIC REVIVAL COTTAGE

c. 1856: Buffalo, New York

After the Erie Canal was completed in 1825, Buffalo grew apace and swelled to encompass some acreage that belonged to L.F. Allen, a Yankee land-speculator who busied himself with genteel farming while waiting for the city to beat a path to his door. In due course, his twenty-nine acre farm became "Allentown," a mostly residential neighborhood in which mansions and cottages alike arose in the last half of the nineteenth century.

Of the survivors from this period, one of the most intriguing is this Gothic Revival cottage, "the most unlikely and wonderful single residence in the City of Buffalo," to quote the Allentown Association.

It is thought to have been built when a portion of the area was subdivided in 1856, and it seems to be one of a pair of identical mirror twins that stood side by side facing onto a neighborhood green called Arlington Park. At some point in the late nineteenth century, the other house was apparently remodeled to reflect the Italianate style, but this one retains much of its original flavor.

It was constructed by Richard Hatch, a stairbuilder, who endowed it with the steep gables, board-and-batten siding, and squared-off label molds that were signatures of the Carpenter's Gothic style. The porch, along with its turned posts, spindle course, and scroll-cut openwork, was added to the house in the 1880s. And it seems likely that the unusual molded bargeboards that adorn the front gable may also have been added at that time. Located improbably near the heart of New York's second largest city, this paradigm of rural Gothic values is still in use as a private residence.

McINDOE-PERKINS HOUSE
1847-48: Windsor, Vermont

Relatively few Gothic Revival houses made it through the nineteenth century without picking up a few new frills along the way. This example shows some decorative acquisitions characteristic of the late Victorian period. The patterned shingles and the pagoda-like canopy over the front porch were probably added in the 1890s. And the cut-out trefoil patterning in the upper and lower balustrades—an echo of the three-cornered window in the gable— seems to be even more recent.

In basic form however, the cottage is a gabled-roof approximation of some of the same structural ideas seen in the hip-roofed Delamater and Brooks houses (pp. 15, 25). Some of the details—steep gables, decorative bargeboards, lancet windows and diamond-shaped panes—are also similar.

The house was built by Sarah Townsend, the widow of Isaac Townsend, a Boston jeweler who arrived in Windsor in 1803. After buying up several parcels of land, he died and left everything to his wife. Thirty-five years later she built a new house in the Gothic Revival style. It was, some townsfolk alleged, the death of her. For after it was assessed at $1200, Sarah Townsend promptly passed away.

In the early 1860s the house was purchased for two thousand dollars by Lyman J. McIndoe, who published a number of periodicals including *The Vermont Chronicle* and *The Vermont Journal*. Later it passed to his daughter, Clara, who married marsh Perkins of Rutland, whence the other half of the name. In recent years, the house has been restored, and it is now in use as a residence and bed & breakfast inn.

REMINGTON-BORDEN HOUSE

1858: Fall River, Massachusetts

Fall River was founded about 1811, but its most dramatic growth occurred in the period from the late 1840s to the 1870s. Its abundant waterpower—a gift from the Quequechan River—made it a perfect site for cotton spinning mills. By 1875, with more than 120 plants, it was one of the leading textile centers in the country.

In time, however, the industry declined and the Great Depression of the 1930s killed off most of Fall River's mills. Although most of them are gone today, the town retains a fine selection of Victorian houses from the era when it was known as "Spindle City."

Most of these survivors are located in the Highlands Historical District which is set on a lofty bluff overlooking the rest of the town. This neighborhood was the preferred site for the homes of local mill-owners during Fall River's heyday. Joseph Remington, who built the house shown here, was one of three brothers who supplied the cotton manufactories with oils, starches, and—in his case—acids. The house was sold in 1864 to Richard A. Borden, a director of one of the mills and the cousin of the Andrew J. Borden who allegedly received forty-one whacks from his ax-wielding daughter Lizzie.

A late bloomer, the house, has most of the features associated with the Gothic Revival style: sharp gables, pointed and quatrefoil windows, and icicle gable decoration similar to the trim that decorates the Justin Smith Morrill House (p. 23). It is also interesting for the classical revival additions it acquired around the turn of the century—the extended veranda with its paired, classical posts, for example. In perfect repair, the house is now used as a summer residence.

43

MELE HOUSE

c. 1855: Baltimore, Maryland

This large cottage in the Gothic Revival style was erected in Mount Washington, a community in the lower Jones Falls Valley about five miles from the heart of Baltimore. Originally a mill town called Washingtonville, it became attractive to residential developers after rail links to the city were established. In the mid-1850s a group of boosters promoted it as the "Mount Washington Rural Retreat," and it soon developed as a summer colony for well-to-do city dwellers. After the Civil War, it became a year-round bedroom community populated mostly by rail commuters.

Although some of its decorative details indicate a later date of construction, the Mele house is thought to be one of the summer cottages that were built during Mount Washington's early period as a rustic retreat. Its highly ornamental character is certainly consistent with this theory.

Though organized symmetrically, the house is quite irregular and "picturesque" in the nineteenth-century sense of the term. It also displays a range of florid details including heavy, bracketed bargeboards and jerkinhead dormers which echo the lines of the main roof. In addition, scroll-cut openwork helps tie the various parts of the house together. The wall surfaces that can be seen behind all this busy detail are sheathed with vertical boards sealed with battens.

All in all, the house represents the Gothic Revival style in a more highly ornamental form than was common in the time of Davis and Downing. Unfortunately, no one seems to know who designed it.

LESLEY-TRAVERS MANSION
c. 1855: New Castle, Delaware

New Castle, the oldest town in the Delaware Valley, was originally a Swedish settlement called Fort Casimir but was renamed Nieu Amstel when the Dutch took over in 1651. The redoubtable Peter Stuyvesant had ambitions to make it a seat of Dutch power on the Delaware comparable to his own Nieu Amsterdam on the Hudson, but annexation by the British put an end to that dream. The town prospered for much of the eighteenth century, but it was occupied by the British during the Revolution and nearly destroyed by fire during the War of 1812. Railroad service between the Delaware and Chesapeake Bays was established in 1832, but at midcentury the line was rerouted to Wilmington, neatly bypassing New Castle. The resulting seclusion has tended to preserve the town's Colonial, Federal, and Victorian architecture.

This structure, an interesting Gothic style villa, was built for Dr. Allen Voorhees Lesley. Though both his father and grandfather had been cabinetmakers, Lesley (1822-1881) distinguished himself as a surgeon. He is remembered for his early use of such innovations as anaesthesia and the microscope, but in those early days, the quick, deft use of the knife and saw was most crucial in his profession, so perhaps the family trade served him in good stead.

Born and raised in Philadelphia, Lesley married and moved to New Castle in 1844. Eleven years later he engaged the Baltimore architects Thomas and James Dixon to design a large residence for his then extensive estate. The house that resulted combined a rambling, almost Italianate plan with such Gothic details as bargeboards and pointed windows.

The house was executed by Augustin Van Kirk of Salem, New Jersey. According to a list of specifications that has survived, it was originally equipped with gas lights, central heating, doorbells, and speaker tubes—all brand new in the mid-1850s. It also had hot and cold running water supplied from a two-hundred gallon *lead-lined* water tank in the loft. The exterior brick walls are hollow, the sills and hood molds are cast iron, and the bargeboards are of wood.

After Lesley's death, the mansion changed hands several times, and by the middle of the present century it had deteriorated rather badly. Restored in recent years, it is now in use as an apartment house.

MOSES BULKELEY HOUSE

1861: Southport, Connecticut

Originally part of Fairfield, Connecticut, Southport began to flourish as an independent seafaring village after the Revolution. Though the British had burned it to the ground in 1779, reconstruction was a relatively simple task since there were only about nine houses to replace. By 1803, however, Southport had dozens of residences and four shipyards, and by the middle of the century it was a small but thriving port. In the meantime it had become home to scores of merchant shippers, sea captains, even a few privateers.

The house shown here was built, probably as a summer home, for Captain Moses Bulkeley, one of a prosperous family of shippers. His father, Eleazar Bulkeley, had been born in Southport in 1763 and went to sea for the first time at the age of twelve—just before the Revolution. After acquiring a thorough, practical knowledge of ships, sailing, and commerce, he married, sired six sons, and started his own merchant shipping company—E. Bulkeley & Sons—which was eventually headquartered in New York City.

The house his son Moses built seems to have been designed by architects Henry A. Lambert and Rufus W. Bunnell, who were active in the Bridgeport area in the 1860s and '70s. According to Bunnell's diary, they received $112.00 for designing the Bulkeley House. The plan is thought to have been executed by the Northrop Brothers, local contractors credited with several churches and some of the fancier houses in town.

As originally constructed, the cottage was cruciform in plan, with a gable-front main wing. The pointed windows and ornate bargeboards are in the tradition of Davis and Downing and are assumed to be part of the original construction. Some of the other details are of a later date. According to the *Southport Chronicle*, the tower was added in 1886, and other unspecified alterations were made in the 1890s. Despite these late Victorian accretions, however, the house retains its original Gothic flavor.

After Moses Bulkeley died in 1869, the house passed to his brother, and, later, to his son, Oliver. Today it is still a private residence, one of a number of well-maintained nineteenth-century structures in the Southport Historical District.

J.B. McCREARY HOUSE, *THE ABBEY*

1869-70: Cape May, New Jersey

Cape May was named for Captain Cornelius Jacobson Mey, a Dutch seafarer who rounded the southern tip of New Jersey in 1620. During the eighteenth century a whaling station was established on the Cape and a small settlement developed; but it was not until the early 1800s that the town began to flourish. After a steamboat line linked it with Philadelphia in 1819, Cape May became popular as a summer vacation spot. Large hotels and rooming houses soon appeared, and before long the town was billing itself as "Queen of the Seaside Resorts."

That appellation may have had some justification in the first half of the century, but after the 1850s Cape May's supremacy was challenged when railroads encouraged travel to more remote resorts. In addition the town suffered a series of devastating fires in the latter half of the nineteenth century. And local voters did nothing to enhance its popularity with tourists when they elected to make it dry in 1890.

Repeated efforts in the waning decades of the century to modernize Cape May's architecture and resort facilities foundered because the wealthy Philadelphians who controlled the town preferred to keep it a quiet vacation community. To the despair of turn-of-the-century boosters Cape May failed to develop into another Atlantic City. But to the delight of recent visitors its late-nineteenth-century character remains largely intact. Today much of the town is a National Historic District in which more than six hundred Victorian and Edwardian structures are preserved.

One of the more interesting survivors is the former summer home of John B. McCreary, a Pennsylvania coal baron and state senator. It was designed by Stephen Decatur Button (1813-1897), a Philadelphia architect who had a strong influence on Cape May's built environment. Originally from Connecticut, Button apprenticed with several architectural firms, then struck off on his own and worked in the South for several years before establishing a practice in Philadelphia in 1848. For the next two decades he was one of the favorite architects of the city's businessmen, several of whom engaged him to design hotels and summer homes in Cape May.

His influence on the resort town's architecture extended beyond his own designs, however. Over the years he worked with most of the local carpenters and builders, and—as George Thomas has pointed out—they seem to have absorbed his generally conservative design principles.

For Button, whose own taste ran towards a somewhat formal version of the Italianate, the McCreary house was an uncharacteristic foray into the Victorian Gothic style. Besides such eclectic details as the sixty-foot corner tower with its exaggerated mansard roof, the house has a profusion of incunabula from the Gothic Revival period: lancet-arched windows, serpentine bargeboards, hood and label molds. As originally constructed by contractor Richard J. Dobbins—another Philadelphian—it also had board-and-batten siding. In the 1890s, however, the battens were removed and clapboard sheathing was applied directly over the vertical boards.

In the 1970s the house served for a time as a Christian Science Church, but more recently it has become *The Abbey*, a bed & breakfast establishment. It is now furnished with Victorian antiques and artifacts, and the first floor is available for tours by the public.

51

EDWARD KING HOUSE

1845: Newport, Rhode Island

Richard Upjohn, who designed *Kingscote* (p. 11), was also responsible for this prototypical Italianate villa. It was built for Edward King, China trader and scion of a prominent Rhode Island family and was executed during Upjohn's New England period, a few years before he established his New York City office. It now serves the City of Newport as a social center.

Though constructed at a relatively early date, the house precociously displayed most of the features that came to be identified with the Italianate villa style—low-pitched roofs, ornamental eaves brackets, round-headed windows, balconies, and hoods. Its true novelty, however, lay in its irregular plan and organization. Based on English picturesque models—which in turn had been derived from vernacular Italian farmhouses—the King House was essentially a group of rectilinear blocks arranged for effect and convenience. This "mid-century experiment in the composition of freely developed masses"—as Vincent Scully, Jr. called it—signaled that the American house was beginning to break out of its boxy past.

Probably because it was one of the villas featured in *The Architecture of Country Houses* (1852), the design proved to be quite influential in generating a taste for the Italianate style. Soon after the book was released, identical houses arose in Maryland and Virginia. And less explicit imitations of the design continued to appear for decades in various parts of the country. Downing's high praise may have had something to do with its popularity. "It is," he wrote, "one of the most successful specimens of the Italian style in the United States, and unites beauty of form and expression with spacious accommodations, in a manner not often seen, and is very creditable to Mr. Upjohn."

If he had continued designing residences like this one, Upjohn might have rivaled Alexander Jackson Davis as the reigning house architect in the era before the Civil War. But as Wayne Andrews has pointed out, Upjohn "...was not an architect who happened to be an Episcopalian, but an Episcopalian who happened to be an architect." Though he published a book of plans for houses in 1852, his residential work was gradually relegated to second and third place as he increasingly devoted his considerable talents to the design of Gothic Revival churches.

Figure 5: "Villa in the Italian Style," from *The Architecture of Country Houses.*

CAPTAIN WILLIAM FIFE HOUSE
Pembroke, New Hampshire

William Fife, for whom this house is named, was born in 1821, the descendant of English and Scottish forbears who had arrived in New Hampshire shortly before the outbreak of the Revolutionary War. His father had combined farming and carpentry to make a living, and Fife followed this lead. At the age of nineteen he struck out on his own and established himself as a builder-contractor. His captaincy derives from a stint in the New Hampshire State Militia.

The house, which has been dated as early as 1847, was apparently built by Fife as his own residence. Of wood-frame construction, it is clad with so-called rusticated siding—wooden panels cut and chamfered to imitate stone blocks.

In style it is basically Italianate but contains a few elements left over from the Greek Revival. The grooved pilasters at the corners are the most obvious of these, but the narrow rectangular widows, or "lights," that frame the door are also Greek. Italianate features include a flat-roofed corner tower, full-arched windows, and ornamental brackets beneath the eaves and cornices. The heavy window hoods with their prominent keystones are high-style details, and the consoles that support the marquee over the front entrances are unusually massive and ornate.

ZEBULON LATIMER HOUSE
1852: Wilmington, North Carolina

Set in the midst of swampy pine barrens at the mouth of the Cape Fear River, Wilmington prospered as North Carolina's principal deepwater port almost from its founding in 1739. Although the Revolutionary War temporarily halted its economic progress, the town quickly recovered after Independence. Railroad links to Raleigh increased its importance in the nineteenth century, and during the Civil War it actually flourished as the Confederacy's major port. In the last half of the nineteenth century and into the twentieth its growth was steady but slow, and it thus avoided the dramatic urban facelifts that most northern port cities experienced in the same period. Today Wilmington retains a good sampling of early buildings including some designed by well-known architects—John Norris, Samuel Sloan, and Richard Upjohn among them.

The house shown here was built for Zebulon Latimer, a Connecticut Yankee who arrived in Wilmington in the 1830s and established a dry goods store. This eventually provided him with the means to become a banker. After his death in 1881, his house passed through a succession of hands until it was purchased in 1967 by the Lower Cape Fear Historical Society. It now serves as the Society's headquarters and as a house museum open to the public.

The design, as well as the construction, is credited to James F. Post, a local builder who worked with several out-of-town architects when they had projects in Wilmington. Essentially a transitional box, the house contains just a few references to the Italianate style that was becoming popular in the early 1850s. The flat roof, decorative cornice brackets, and pedimented window hoods are characteristic of the style, and the coigned cornerboards are consistent with it. The front porch with its neoclassical posts and turned balusters seems to have been added later in the century, but the side porch with its delicate iron filigree was part of the original construction.

57

THOMAS RUSSELL HOUSE

1873: Thomaston, Maine

One of the picture-postcard towns that dot Maine's central coast like pearls on a string, Thomaston began as an Indian trading post and was formally founded by English settlers in 1736. Since the nineteenth century it has changed only slightly. Its surviving historical architecture includes the usual Georgian and Federal examples with an occasional Johnny-come-lately from the Victorian period thrown in for good measure.

One of the latter, the Russell House of the early 1870s, has managed to uphold the prim standards of traditional New England building while flirting with some new ideas imported from Italy. Its basic form is the cube, a shape that transcended changing fashion and kept reappearing in new guises throughout the nineteenth century. Still in use as a private residence, the house was built by a carpenter named Thomas Russell as a wedding gift for his wife.

To the basic builder's box Russell added a few graceful stylistic notes, some old, some new. On the traditional side are the hipped roof, window shutters, and coigned corner boards—all of which seem to be survivals from the Georgian period. Some of the other details, however, indicate a provisional exploration of the Italianate style.

The extreme regularity of the facade—another bow to tradition—is broken by the off-center entryway which provides a touch of asymmetry. The three sets of brackets that nominally support the eaves also point to the Italianate, as do the small hoods over the windows. These details, however, are modest and restrained by comparison with more flamboyant representatives of the style. The most daring feature displayed here is the small lookout tower, or belvedere, at the apex of the low-pitched roof. Here, high up and inconspicuous, are more brackets, round-headed windows, and a jauntily curved pyramidal cap.

GOVERNOR ROSS HOUSE

c. 1855: Seaford, Delaware

"There is a strong and growing partiality among us for the Italian style," wrote A.J. Downing in his *Country Houses*. "Originally adapted to the manifestation of social life, in a climate almost the counterpart of that of the Middle and Southern portions of our country. . .it is made to conform exactly to our tastes and habits. . .Its broad roofs, ample verandas and arcades, are especially agreeable in our summers of dazzling sunshine. . ."

The Italian Villa, he went on to say, was inferior to the Gothic Cottage as a style for country houses; but he thought it admirably suited to "expressing the elegant culture and variety of accomplishment of the retired citizen or man of the world."

Governor William Ross (1814-1887) was just such a man, and probably thought of himself as one. He was a little over forty when he built this villa-style residence, but he was already wealthy, accomplished, well read, and sophisticated by travel. In his younger days he had been one of the first men in the southern part of Delaware to develop extensive peach orchards and had prospered nicely from his efforts. Moreover, in 1850 he had become governor at the age of thirty-six, the youngest in the history of the state.

While in Dover he had used his influence to bring the railroad to Seaford; and a few years after leaving office he built his retirement residence not far from the new tracks.

Constructed of brick with a covering of stucco, the house was one of the first manifestations of the Italianate style in Delaware. Basically an arrangement of wings around a dominant tower, it was embellished with most of the accouterments that define the style: round-headed windows with hood molds, brackets beneath the cornices, low-pitched roofs. The arcaded porch Downing mentions is here, too. No record has survived to indicate the source of the design, but it might well have been taken from one of the pattern books of the day. Today the Ross House serves as headquarters for the Seaford Historical Society.

61

MAYHURST
1859-60: Orange, Virginia

This plantation house in the Tuscan style was built by Colonel John Willis, a nephew of President James Madison, whose own residence, Montpelier, was not far away. *Mayhurst* was the focal point of an 880-acre estate that Willis bought in 1856. Completed just before the Civil War broke out, it served in the winter of 1863-64 as headquarters for General A.P. Hill of the Army of Northern Virginia. Far from the scene of any major engagement, it is remembered as the setting of a happy moment in the midst of the conflict. Hill's infant daughter was baptized there with Robert E. Lee standing as her godfather.

Who designed *Mayhurst* is not recorded, but houses of this sort were not uncommon in the South in the late antebellum period. Like Camden (p. 65), it is an Italianate version of the classically-inspired plantation houses that were one of the mainstays of southern architecture in the first half of the nineteenth century. Formally balanced examples like this one were sometimes called Tuscan to distinguish them from the more rambling and picturesque Italianate villa. The Tuscan villa retained some of the formality and classical balance of the older Greek style while bringing a new sophisticated touch to the southern plantation house.

In addition, some of its features suited it admirably to the climate. Thick walls helped insulate the interior from the outside heat; high ceilings, central staircases, and transoms over the bedroom doors promoted air circulation; and the cupola—far from being a merely decorative fixture—drew warm air through the roof like a chimney. On the outside of the house, overhanging eaves provided shade that classical roofs could not, and tall windows brought an abundance of light into the interior apartments. Masonry construction seems to have been rare in such houses. Most were built on heavy timber frames sheathed with flushboard, or—as in this example—wooden panels cut to look like stone blocks.

Today *Mayhurst* is listed on the National Register and has been designated as an Historic Landmark by the State of Virginia. It is currently in use as a bed & breakfast inn.

CAMDEN
1859: Port Royal, Virginia

"The southern gentleman," wrote Samuel Sloan, "is not circumscribed in the construction of his house, or the laying out of gardens and lawns..., the number of laborers at his command, the entire year, render him less chary in the indulgence of his taste...than he would be if [it]...required a constant drain on his purse. Instead of building upward, he prefers increasing the area of his ground floor, and having fewer stories to ascend. The climate...does not demand, for the comfort of the inmates, windows with double sashes, and doors set in air-tight frames, and those houses are most suitable whose openings are so constructed as to permit, at pleasure, such an union of rooms and verandahs as to make them almost one and the same apartment. The laws of hospitality, observed there, require a larger number of sleeping apartments ...since at many seasons of the year, the southern householder takes a pride in converting his mansion into a sort of honorary hotel."

Camden is yet another example of the Italianate villa adapted to the requirements of a southern plantation house. It was built by William Carter Pratt, a wealthy landowner whose family and the name *Camden* traces back to England. In 1857 he engaged the Baltimore architect N.G. Starkwether to design a new house to replace the eighteenth-century one he had inherited from his father. Starkwether responded with the design for the fashionable villa shown here.

Square in plan and formal in organization, it nonetheless embodied a new freedom in decorative details that served to distinguish it from the classically-inspired houses of the past. There were paired brackets beneath wide eaves, tall, hooded windows with full and segmental arches, and an extended porch that wrapped the house on three sides. Inside, it was even more up to date. There was indoor plumbing with running water in each bedroom and shower baths as well as tubs. There was also central heating and gaslights, both supplied from a private gas works.

Constructed on a granite foundation and sheathed with cypress flushboard, *Camden* was completed just before the outbreak of the Civil War. Unlike *Mayhurst* (p. 63), however, it did not survive the conflict unscathed. In 1863 a Union gunboat cruising the Rappahannock River opened fire on the house and destroyed the tower that originally topped the structure. No other damage was done, but the tower was never replaced. Now listed on the National Register, *Camden* still serves as the Pratt family residence.

Figure 6: N.G. Starkwether drawing of the W.C. Pratt Residence, from the Library of Congress Collection.

JOHNSTON-HAY HOUSE
1856-60: Macon Georgia

At the beginning of the Victorian era, the classical spirit that informed much of the South's antebellum architecture found new expression in the Italianate style. Among the wealthy, residences based on Italian Renaissance models were particularly favored because they provided much the same scale and aristocratic demeanor that marked the old Greek Revival plantation houses. In contrast to the rambling villas of the bracketed Italian style, Renaissance houses retained the formal symmetry of earlier southern mansions and made free use of classical as well as Italianate details.

Some of this is illustrated in the Johnston-Hay House, the most elaborate antebellum survivor in Macon. It was originally the home of William B. Johnston, a wealthy Georgia businessman, who built it shortly after he and his bride returned home from a honeymoon in Italy. It was completed just in time for the War Between the States, and during the siege of Macon in July, 1864 it narrowly escaped being destroyed by Union artillery.

The design is attributed to T. Thomas & Son of New York, but to complicate matters, James B. Ayers, a Macon builder originally from New Jersey, is listed as architect on some of the surviving records. Thomas was a transplanted English architect who had done some work for the Astors and gets half credit for St. Peter's Church in Manhattan.

Though the house breaks into wings at the rear, the organization of the facade is quite formal and symmetrical. Broad marble steps converge onto a semicircular portico tied to a full-width porch on which Corinthian columns support a second-story balcony. The windows are mostly round headed in the Italian manner, and those on the second floor are set off with elaborate surrounds capped alternately with arched and triangular pediments. On the roof is an octagonal cupola with circular windows, enormous scroll brackets, and a balustrade all its own. Inside the house, the lavish trappings include panels in oak and rosewood, extremely elaborate stucco ceilings, a carved mahogany staircase, black and white marble floors, and a fifty-foot ballroom with a coved ceiling thirty feet high. All in all, it was a palace worthy of the very wealthy Mr. Johnston.

William Makepeace Thackeray, of all people, had met him in Macon while the house was still abuilding, and he noted in a letter home that "Johnstone" owned a shop and that he was very rich. He got the second part right at least. Johnston may have owned a shop but he also owned a bank, and the Macon Manufacturing company, and more. And more. During the Civil War he was a principal in the Confederate Depository in Macon, and it was this sinecure, doubtless, that inspired the rumor that he had a fortune in rebel gold hidden in a secret room in his mansion.

Maybe he did, for after the war he continued to prosper as before. Despite the general financial ruin in Georgia, he was soon helping rebuild some of the railroad lines Sherman's army had torn up, and before long he had established himself as the President of the Cotton States Life Insurance Company.

Just like Mrs. Winchester in California, Johnston is supposed to have entertained the superstition that he would die once the house was completed and so left a piece of iron fencing undone—a stratagem that kept the reaper at bay until 1886.

The mansion remained in the possession of his family until 1925 when it was purchased by another insurance man, Park Lee Hay, who thought it would make a dandy setting for the art treasures he had collected over the years. He and his wife gathered the sumptuous furnishings that now fill the house, which is open for public tours.

RYERSS MANSION, BURHOLME
1859: Philadelphia, Pennsylvania

This imposingly formal Italianate mansion was originally the country seat of Joseph Waln Ryerss, who named the estate *Burholme*—"Briar Hill"—after his family's ancestral home in England. Ryerss had made his considerable fortune in the China and East Indies trade and later extended his holdings to include railroads, including the Tioga, of which he was president. He died in 1868, and the house and grounds passed to his son, Robert W. Ryerss, an attorney and restless globetrotter who gathered a library of rare books and a collection of Oriental artifacts during his extensive travels.

Originally built as a summer house in the Foxcroff section of Philadelphia, *Burholme* became a full-time residence in the mid-1870s when the suburban railroad made commuting to the city practical. Some additions were made to the rear of the house at that time: the prominent cupola, however, was added in the early 1890s.

In other respects the house stands today as originally built. In plan it is practically square, with the front facade organized in strict symmetry. The central gable that often dominated formal Italianate houses has here become a semicircular arch—a feature that is occasionally seen in some other Italianate houses that have survived from the late 1850s. The cornice—another unusual feature—is supported by plain, rectangular modillions instead of the heavily carved brackets common in such houses. All of these details are of wood, but the main construction material is roughcast stone covered with stucco, and the low-pitched hipped roof is of tin. Unfortunately, no records have survived to tell us who designed and built the mansion.

In his will, Robert Ryerss specified that after his widow's death the estate be deeded to the City of Philadelphia for use as a park, library, and museum "free to the people forever." In keeping with this wish, the house now serves as a museum and branch library.

EBENEZER MAXWELL MANSION

1859: Philadelphia, Pennsylvania

With the coming of the railroad in the mid-nineteenth century, Germantown, an independent village founded in 1683 by Dutch and German settlers, became one of Philadelphia's first suburbs. Sometime in the late 1850s Ebenezer Maxwell, a rising middle-class textile merchant and an enthusiastic apostle of the gospel of country living, visited the place and decided that it would be an ideal and moral environment in which to raise a family. Not long afterwards he moved his wife and children there, began commuting to work by rail, and built this expansive stone villa—not as a permanent residence, mind, but as a speculative project. He occupied the mansion only a year or two before selling it to build another, presumably less ostentatious house nearby.

No records have yet surfaced to tell us who designed this extraordinary castle-like house, but it could have been any one of a number of architects working in Philadelphia in the late 1850s. Similar designs had even appeared in pattern books. But this particular house is extraordinary in its combination of elements appropriated from various styles. The castellated porch with its rounded arches is Norman, the tower, Italianate; and the roof is an early version of the mansard that became a hallmark of the French Second Empire Style a decade later. In addition, the roof dormers with their shaped gables are idiosyncratic and quite remarkable.

The construction material was a local stone—Wissahickon schist—which was rough cut, laid up in free courses, and bound with mortar mixed with coal dust and quartz sand. The diamond-shaped inserts, which add order and color to the facade, are of red sandstone. The cornices, window sills, and lintels are of wood, sand painted to simulate masonry. When new, the house was equipped with gas lights, hot and cold running water, and central heating supplied by a coal furnace.

After its last private owner passed away in the late 1960s, ingenuous developers suggested razing the mansion to make room for a new gasoline station. Local outrage, however, put an end to this plan and got the house certified by the Philadelphia Historical Commission. It was later added to the National Register of Historic Places. Restored and refurbished by volunteers, the Maxwell Mansion was opened to the public in 1975. Today it serves as a Victorian House Museum and library and contains materials on "nineteenth-century history, lifestyle and architecture, historic preservation, and restoration techniques."

W.B. WARD HOUSE

c. 1860s: Richfield Springs, New York

The European custom of taking the waters took a while to reach the New World but when it did, it quickly became fashionable. By the mid-1700s Americans were enduring uncomfortable stagecoach trips and primitive accommodations in order to bask in the natural hot springs that seem to occur only in remote locations.

The soaking was only part of the cure, however. In the early days at least, a major objective of attending a spa was to induce a purge—the more violent and complete, the better. Prevailing medical opinion held that if it didn't kill the patient, it was probably good for what ailed him. Later, however, distinct social overtones attended visits to spas and more genteel sipping and soaking supplanted the purgative side of the experience.

At the end of the eighteenth century Richfield Springs-to-be was little more than a gristmill and tavern on the site of a natural sulphur spring thirty-five miles from Utica. But in 1808 the Western Turnpike was routed through town, and local entrepreneurs soon began entertaining ideas of exploiting the spring as a medicinal attraction. Richfield began to develop as a spa as early as the 1820s, but it was not until the Delaware, Lackawanna, and Western ran a branch line into town in 1870 that it began to take off as a fashionable summer resort. For the next few decades it was one of the preferred stops on an upstate circuit that also included Saratoga and Sharon Springs. At its height the town boasted a bathing pavilion, roller rink, racetrack, velodrome, four newspapers, and at least ten hotels, some of them fine and fancy indeed.

Though Richfield never seriously rivaled Saratoga Springs for the title of "Queen of the Spas," it was at least known as a contender in the last decades of the nineteenth century. After 1900, however, it began to decline as a resort town. By that time the centuries-old fad of taking the waters was beginning to wane as modern medical theories debunked the old notions. Saratoga, which had its famous racetrack and an unparalleled social scene, was able to maintain some vestiges of its former glory in the twentieth century; but Richfield, beset with aging hotels and reduced rail service, returned to its original status as a quiet country village.

As a legacy of its late-nineteenth-century past, however, a number of Victorian houses are still standing in town. The sophisticated Shingle style summer home that McKim, Mead, and White designed for Cyrus McCormack has been demolished, but the town retains some other distinguished examples—*Stansfield Villa* and the *Hinds House* notably. Of the house pictured here little is known except the name of its first owner. It was apparently built as a summer home, but even this is not certain. The style is Italianate as evidenced by the central tower, bracketed cornices, and segmental-arched windows with ornate crowns. Recently restored, it is once again in use as a summer home.

E.H. HOLLISTER HOUSE
1864: Rochester, New York

Rochester's beginnings trace back to the late eighteenth century when a pair of Yankee traders bought 2.5 million acres of Lake Ontario and Genesee River land from the Seneca Indians. Later, in 1811, a developer named Colonel Nathaniel Rochester bought the site just below the upper falls of the Genesee and gave his name to the town that grew up around the mills that tapped this ready source of power. After the Erie canal was completed in 1825, canal boats began arriving in Rochester with loads of lumber, potash, and prodigious quantities of Midwestern wheat—grist for the mills that soon made the city "The Flour Capital of the Nation."

In the 1850s, Rochester's third ward—known also as "Corn Hill"—emerged as the premier residential district in town. Bounded by the river and the canal, it was a convenient location for the homes of mill owners, merchants, and other businessmen. After the turn of the century, however, the area began to decline; and by the 1950s it had all the earmarks of an urban slum.

Some of the neighborhood had already been lost to highways, civic development, and urban renewal when the city and the Landmarks Society stepped in to create a preservation district in the 1960s. Since then, much of the area has been rejuvenated and—yes—gentrified; but as a result of these efforts, many of Rochester's early houses have been saved.

Today Corn Hill comprises many blocks of nineteenth-century residences, mostly brick, in styles that range from the Federal to the Queen Anne. This house, which has lately been converted into an apartment building, originally belonged to a lumber merchant named Emmett H. Hollister. Who designed it can only be conjectured, but it exemplifies the Italianate villa style in a suburban mode. The plan seen here—an L-shaped arrangement of cross-gabled wings flanking a central tower—was very common in such houses. Variations on the same theme can be seen in the Pink House (p. 77) and the Morse-Libby Mansion (p. 79).

E.B. HALL HOUSE, *THE PINK HOUSE*
1868: Wellsville, New York

The area around Wellsville in the southern tier of New York State was pioneered in 1791, but local settlers didn't get around to founding a town formally until the early 1830s. As the story goes, a group of them convened one day and named the budding community after Gardner Wells, the only local citizen not in attendance.

In due course a branch line of the Erie Railroad was routed through the area, and in 1852, not long after its completion, a young man from Connecticut stepped off the train and opened a drugstore in Wellsville. This was Edwin Bradford Hall (1825-1903), the descendant of a family whose roots traced back to the Plymouth Colony. The pharmacy he ran for the next half century was evidently quite successful, and he is said to have enhanced his fortune with shrewd deals in whiskey and Allegany crude oil; but he is chiefly remembered for some odd scientific discoveries and for the flamboyant residence he built for himself and his family.

An amateur paleontologist, Hall gathered fossil sponges for nearly fifty years and amassed more than five-thousand specimens. This important collection was eventually acquired by the Carnegie Museum in Pittsburgh. But he also attained a measure of scientific immortality when he discovered a previously unclassified species, known today as *Dictyophyton halli.*

As for his house, it is supposed to have been inspired by a villa that Hall and his wife saw while honeymooning in the Lake Como region of Italy. He is said to have designed it himself, but it seems clear that he got at least some professional help before beginning construction.

A receipt from the firm of Henry Searle & Son, Architects, shows that in May, 1865 Hall paid $125.00 for plans, elevations, specifications and working drawings for a "dwelling house." To the receipt the architect added a short note: "I am glad you are pleased with the plans and will soon complete the remainder of the ornament."

Searle (1809-1892) was originally from Springfield, Massachusetts and had apprenticed with Ammi B. Young of Boston. Later in his career he worked in the office of the U.S. Supervising Architect in Washington, D.C. But from 1844 until 1867 he was active in Rochester, where some of his work is still standing.

In plan and organization, *The Pink House*, as it is known, is a textbook example of the Italianate villa style. The carved and flat-cut gingerbread, however, is unusually ornate by comparison with other surviving examples of the style, and the cornice brackets that usually mark Italianate houses are oddly missing here. In other respects, however, the house is true to type. Essentially an arrangement of wings and bays around a central block and tower, it is rambling and asymmetric but nicely balanced. Of wood-frame construction, the house is clad with flushboard siding. And by all accounts it has been painted the same shade of pink ever since it was first built. After 120 years, it still serves Hall's descendants as a private residence.

MORSE-LIBBY HOUSE, *VICTORIA MANSION*
1858-60: Portland, Maine

Good examples of houses in the Italianate style can still be found in many parts of the United States, particularly in small towns and in the suburbs. But the most extravagant expressions of the style—expansive city dwellings in brick and stone—have mostly succumbed to urban development. An exception is this imposing mansion, originally the summer home of Ruggles Sylvester Morse, a wealthy hotel owner.

Morse (1816-93), was from the small hamlet of Leeds, Maine, but in his youth he left the family farm behind and acquired a solid knowledge of upscale innkeeping working in hotels in Boston, New York, and New Orleans. His career was interrupted by the 1849 gold rush, but by 1851 he was back in New Orleans where he acquired the first of several hotels that he operated in the city for the next three decades. In time his Louisiana interests also included a mortgage company, a sugar plantation, and a pharmaceuticals concern. In the 1880s, however, he left the South and retired to Maine and the Italianate house that he had built some years before.

Following his death, the mansion was acquired by another late-nineteenth-century entrepreneur, the walrus-mustached Joseph Ralph Libby, owner of Portland's largest department store. Libby was one of the new breed of retailers who replaced the old-fashioned general store with gigantic, centralized shopping emporiums in the last decades of the nineteenth century. He claimed to have "the best goods at the bottomest prices," and his awareness of the power of scale and display were on the order of P.T. Barnum's. He bought Morse's conspicuous house for, it is said, twenty cents on the dollar.

On the evidence of recently-discovered building specifications bearing his name, the house is now credited to Henry Austin, the New Haven architect who also designed *Villa Vista* (p. 169). Austin was known for his Italianate house designs, and of these the Morse-Libby is a worthy representative. The exterior demonstrates his cool mastery of the form and his ability to impart new power and elegance to ideas that had already been thoroughly explored by the time this house was built. Some remnants of his earliest work in the Greek Revival style are evident in such classical details as the Ionic columns that front the facade. But high-style Italianate details—ornamental quoins and elaborate window surrounds with carved brackets and pediments—are also in evidence.

The house is constructed of brick faced with brownstone, the Northeast's abundant, cost-effective answer to marble. The dark stone that covers the Morse-Libby house was quarried in Connecticut, but perhaps carelessly, for it shows the cumulative effects of 130 Maine winters. A project to repair and restore the facing is currently underway.

Even if the exterior were reduced to naked brick, however, the elaborate interiors alone would justify the repeated claim that this house is the finest representative of the Italianate villa style still standing in America. The decor, which has been attributed to the designer Gustave Herter, is sumptuous indeed, and the grain paintings on some of the ceilings are exceptionally fine. *Victoria Mansion*, as the house is now known, is open to the public for tours under the auspices of the Victoria Society of Maine.

BENJAMIN WEBSTER HOUSE
1880: Portsmouth, New Hampshire

Portsmouth, or "Strawbery Banke," as it was first called, was founded in 1630. In its earliest years fishing and farming sustained the town, but its fine harbor soon made it a contender in the West Indies trade, and the ready availability of timber led it inevitably to shipbuilding. The latter industry persisted as the cornerstone of the local economy until well into the nineteenth century and exerted a continual pull on Yankee farm boys who came to the city looking for work.

One of the most successful of these backwoods artisans was Benjamin Franklin Webster (1824-1916), who arrived in Portsmouth from Epsom at the age of seventeen. He began his career as a carpenter's apprentice, later worked as a ships joiner, and eventually established his own construction company. By the 1860s he was winning major building contracts and was responsible for the construction of a number of schools and hotels as well as some of the larger private residences in Portsmouth.

Still later, he branched into real estate. According to a county history published when Webster was in his nineties, he paid $3,500 in property taxes in 1913—a considerable sum in those days—and was accounted one of the wealthiest men in town. His biographer also tells us that he did not use eyeglasses despite his advanced age, and that he was a Unitarian, a "valued member of the Masonic fraternity," and an "ardent and enthusiastic Republican."

On the evidence of an old photograph, the sizeable Italianate mansion Webster built for himself in 1880 has changed remarkably little since the turn of the century. It was designed by Albert C. Fernald, a young architect who appears to have been a native of Portsmouth, though he later practiced in Boston. He was the son of a local lumber dealer, through whom, presumably, he met Webster.

In plan the house is L-shaped with a tower placed at the intersection of the two main wings. Rather atypical of Italianate houses, the relatively steep-pitched roof may have been a concession to the realities of winter in New England. More characteristic of the style are the cornice brackets, pedimented window hoods, and round-headed windows on the upper floors. Though it might pass for masonry, the house is actually constructed of wood. The flush-board siding promotes this illusion and the corner quoins complete the *trompe l'oeil*. In fine repair, Webster's one-time residence is currently in use as a funeral home.

J.K. KENDRICK HOUSE

1867: Providence, Rhode Island

Founded in 1636 by Roger Williams, a minister whose outspoken sermons had gotten him banished from the Massachusetts Colony, Providence was at first an agricultural settlement. After 1700, however, its economic base shifted to shipping and shipbuilding—activities that supported it until after the Revolution. In the nineteenth century, moreover, it began to emerge as a manufacturing center. With the advent of the railroads, the city entered a boom period that reached a crescendo in the decades after the Civil War.

Around midcentury, residential development began to extend westward from the city center along Broadway, one of the main east-west boulevards in town. Despite its relatively small lots, the street became a particular favorite among newly rich industrialists and was soon lined with stylish mansions. One of the most impressive that has survived is the Italianate Villa shown here.

It was originally the residence of John K. Kendrick, owner of the Kendrick Loom Harness Company, and it is said to have cost him about $20,000 to build. In 1881 the house was purchased by George Prentice, a buttonhook manufacturer who later put his money into streetcar development. Some additions to the house may have been made at the time he acquired it. The design is credited to Perez Mason, a Providence architect who is remembered for several other expansive residences in town.

The design incorporates rich Italianate detailing in a structure almost churchlike in its verticality. The upward momentum generated by the four-story tower and tall windows is reinforced graphically by the unusual arrowpoint gables. The structure is interesting in comparison to Stephen Decatur Button's McCreary House in Cape May, New Jersey (p. 51).

FAIRBANKS HOUSE

1885: Fernandina Beach, Florida

Located on Amelia Island north of Jacksonville, Fernandina Beach is one of the oldest resorts in Florida. In 1821 when it became United States territory along with the rest of the peninsula, it was a hotbed of pirates and smugglers. But its pleasant, secluded harbor eventually lured businessmen and tourists as well. Shortly after Florida achieved statehood in 1846, David Levi Yulee, president of the Florida Railroad, purchased property on the island and laid out a town over the site of several Spanish land grants that had been previously consolidated by a ship's captain and planter named Domingo Fernandez. By the 1880s the town was thriving as a railroad and shipping center and winter resort. Today the Fernandina Beach Historical District, which is included in the National Register, comprises nearly thirty blocks of late-nineteenth-century commercial buildings and residences.

One of the latter is the Italianate style house that George Rainsford Fairbanks built in 1885. Originally from Watertown, New York, Fairbanks (1820-1906) had studied law and was admitted to the New York State bar in 1842. However, that same year he relocated to Florida, where the territorial government was offering special inducements to attract talented, educated immigrants from more developed areas of the country.

Settling in Saint Augustine, Fairbanks soon became a state senator and developed a romantic fixation for Florida's Spanish past. In 1857 he helped found the state historical society and later wrote two books on Florida history. He was also active in the citrus industry and at one time served as president of the state Fruit Grower's Association. When the Civil War broke out, he joined the Army of Tennessee, and before the conflict ended he had attained the rank of major.

After Appomattox he built a log house known as "Rebels Rest" at Sewannee, Tennessee, where he helped found the University of the South before returning to Florida. In 1879 he moved to Fernandina Beach, became the editor of *The Florida Mirror*, and, a few years later, built the house shown here.

According to a notice in Fairbanks' paper it was designed by an architect named R.V. Schuyler, who may actually have been a local contractor. The house was built in the Italianate villa style which, though a bit out of fashion by the mid-1880s, was still admirably suited to Florida's subtropical climate. Like earlier villa-style houses it is essentially a group of irregularly massed wings arranged around a central block. Of special note here are the arcaded loggias on two sides of the house and the tall tower from which, according to Fairbanks' daughter, she and her father watched Jacksonville burn in the great fire of 1901. Today the house is in service as an apartment building.

CHATEAU-SUR-MER

1852-72: Newport, Rhode Island

"The place consists, as the reader will know, of an ancient and honorable town, a goodly harbor, and a long, broad neck of land, stretching southward into the sea and forming the chief habitation of the summer colony. Along the greater part of its eastward length, this projecting coast is bordered with cliffs of no great height, and dotted with seaward-gazing villas. At the head of the promontory the villas enjoy a magnificent reach of prospect. The pure Atlantic—the old world westward tides—expire directly at their feet."

Thus Henry James describing Newport, Rhode Island in 1870. One of the villas that enjoyed this "magnificent reach of prospect" was *Chateau-sur-Mer*, built in 1852 but substantially altered and enlarged twenty years later. It was originally the home of William Shepherd Wetmore (1801-1862), who made his fortune in the East Indies trade. In his youth, while in the employ of a shipping firm that belonged to two of his uncles, Wetmore had been shipwrecked off Valparaiso, Chile, where he nevertheless succeeded in making a small fortune. Later, in Canton, China, he increased his nest egg substantially, and, still later, in New York, he became a partner in a very successful import firm. At the age of fifty he retired to Newport and built the basis of the mansion shown here. A decade later he died and left the house and property to his second son.

William Peabody Wetmore (1846-1921) was rich, well educated, and ambitious—a potentially lethal combination—but his star seems to have been a truly lucky one. After graduating from Yale, he took a degree in law from Columbia and was admitted to the bar both in New York and Rhode Island. Some years later he entered politics, serving first as a presidential elector, then as governor, and finally as one of the United States senators representing Rhode Island.

In the meantime he enlarged and remodeled the already substantial house he had inherited from his father. As initially constructed by Seth Bradford, a Newport contractor, it had a hipped gambrel roof with a concave lower slope, a nearly mansardic configuration that gave the house an impressive and imperious air in keeping with its scale and the material of its construction—rough cut Fall River granite.

When Richard Morris Hunt's additions to the mansion were completed, however, it was even more impressive and palatial. His work on the exterior included a new porte-cochere and the addition of extensive wings at the rear of the house. In the front, however, he merely emphasized what was already there, increasing the height of the roof and giving its lower slope a more pronounced and imposing angle. The alterations to the interior were more elaborate and more characteristic of Hunt. His changes included a huge ballroom and galleried central hall with a grand staircase and stained-glass skylight. The interior trappings by Luigi Frullini of Florence were equally lavish.

The Chateau by the sea afforded Hunt, who was soon to become court architect to the Vanderbilts, one of his first opportunities to indulge his taste for enormous rooms and high ceilings. And it set the stage for the even larger and more sumptuous mansions that began to appear in Newport a decade or so later.

In 1969 *Chateau-sur-Mer* was purchased from the Wetmore heirs by the Preservation Society of Newport County. Today it is one of several large villas in town that are open for public tours.

HORATIO MOODY HOUSE
1866: Kennebunk, Maine

Situated between the Mousam and Kennebunk Rivers on Maine's southern coast, the small town of Kennebunk began to develop about 1650. By the 1730s it was enjoying a share of the lucrative West Indies trade and was also engaged in shipbuilding, an industry that sustained it through the troubled era of revolution, embargoes, and impressment at the end of the eighteenth century.

After Independence shipbuilding continued to flourish in Kennebunk. Between 1800 and 1850 nearly one thousand wooden sailing vessels were produced by the fifty-odd shipyards in the immediate area. As the century progressed, however, the industry began to decline. As early as the 1840s local timber was growing scarce, and after the Civil War steel-hulled, steam-powered freighters which required deepwater ports for their construction began to supplant the rakish, full-rigged barks and brigs that has been the mainstays of the town's economy.

Today shipbuilding is just a memory in Kennebunk, but reminders of it can be found in numerous historical homes dating from the Federal, Greek Revival, and Victorian periods. Besides the famous *Wedding Cake House* (p. 29), which was built by a ships carpenter, one of the best-preserved nineteenth-century structures in Kennebunk is the former Moody residence— the first house in town to be built in the French Second Empire style, according to George Gilpatric's *Kennebunk History*.

By comparison with later examples of the style which soon acquired asymmetrical facades, rambling bays, towers, and other Victorian details, this house is quite formal in organization and demeanor. Some of its features, in fact, suggest a transition from an earlier style. The boxy plan, elliptical fanlight at the entry, and heavy applique around the modified Palladian windows are all characteristic of Georgian houses. The flushboard siding was also common in the early nineteenth century. It is mainly the concave mansard roof and the centered cupola which serve to distinguish this house from its predecessors.

Now a funeral parlor, the house was originally the home of Horatio Moody, a "master mariner" who sailed a succession of vessels out of Kennebunkport. He was, however, marked for tragedy. Of one of Moody's voyages in his ship, *Rembrandt*, Gilpatric records the following:

"In the fall of 1876, accompanied by his wife and two sons, he sailed from New York bound for San Francisco around Cape Horn. On the return voyage from San Francisco to Liverpool, in a terrific storm in the Pacific Ocean, May 10, 1877, the two boys were washed overboard and drowned."

FRANCIS WEISS HOUSE

1870: Bethlehem, Pennsylvania

Slouching home from Bethlehem, Mencken wrote: "It is a town founded mainly on steel and it looks appropriately hard and brisk—a town, one guesses instantly, in which Rotarians are not without honor." And yet he liked it for the remnants of "homeliness and rusticity" that he found there, remnants which he attributed to the town's Moravian founders.

Bethlehem had started off in 1741 as a communal village of the Renewed Church of the Brethren, a religious group noted for music and craftsmanship among other things. As a legacy of those beginnings, the town holds an annual Bach Festival and boasts some of the finest prerevolutionary stone buildings still standing in America. But it also shows the effects of the industrialization that overtook it later in its history. In the last half of the nineteenth century the anthracite coal that was so abundant in the area fueled rolling mills and a new industrial-based economy with architecture to match.

The house shown here represents the French Second Empire style that became widely popular in Bethlehem and elsewhere after the Civil War. With their intimations of continental elegance, houses of this sort appealed particularly to the self-made man. A mansard roof atop a house was a flag that signaled its owner's success.

This example was built for Francis Weiss (1820-1889), the grandson of a Virginia surveyor, Colonel Jacob Weiss, who is credited with finding the first anthracite coal beds in eastern Pennsylvania. The discovery, however, seems not to have had any positive effect on his family's fortune. Francis Weiss was a poor boy, the son of a farmer. Nonetheless, he was educated well enough to become a teacher and surveyor.

As a young man he helped build the celebrated "switchback" gravity railroad that ran coal down the mountains to Mauch Chunk (now Jim Thorpe), and in 1860 he established a mining operation that he ran successfully until his lease ran out a decade later. In 1870 he repaired to Bethlehem where he acquired interests in coal mining operations, an iron works, and—not to miss any bets in this one-man version of the triangle trade—a shovel factory. His biographer notes that "He was a straight Republican, but not an aspirant for office." He doesn't say whether or not Weiss was a Rotarian.

Some sense of the scale of the residence he built shortly after moving to town is suggested by the fact that it has been recently converted into five separate condominium units. In many respects it is similar to the Italianate houses of a slightly earlier period. There are the customary brackets beneath the cornice, segmental-arched windows, and a side bay. In this example the facade is symmetrical and rather formal with a central tower and bay that pushes slightly forward from the main body of the house. A freer rendition of some of these same elements can be seen in the Meyers House next door (p. 99).

SECOND EMPIRE HOUSE

c. 1875: Richford, Vermont

     This house near the Canadian Border was originally the home of Silas Pratt Carpenter, a local entrepreneur. Besides business ventures in land and real estate in the Richford area, Carpenter served as the town's treasurer and as the local U.S. Customs Collector.

     Though no hard evidence has survived to confirm the suspicion, the house is believed to have been constructed by local builders. If so, it seems likely that they were working from a stock plan. In any event, the design is quite similar to that of the Weiss House in Bethlehem, Pennsylvania (p. 91). Both structures are organized symmetrically and their facades are dominated by a central bay topped by the mansardic equivalent of a gable. This rather formal arrangement was typical of early Second Empire houses.

     Also of note in the Carpenter House are the contrasting curves of the roof and the incised motifs that appear on the porch and in the window surrounds. In recent years, the house has been restored and converted for use as an office building.

EVANS HOUSE
1882: Salem, Virginia

Western Virginia began to experience its first real development in the early 1880s when the Norfolk and Western linked up with the Shenandoah Valley Railroad at Big Lick, soon to become Roanoke. The mere announcement of the impending merger was enough to set off a wave of speculative expansion in the area, and Salem, Roanoke's smaller neighbor, was swept along in the tide.

The Evans house, one of the residences that arose during this period, is notable as an example of the Second Empire style, which was rare in Virginia and rarer still in the western part of the state. It was built by John M. Evans (1837-1891), a dry goods merchant and prominent citizen of the community. The son of a wealthy Virginia landowner, Evans had served in an artillery company during "The War" and afterwards moved to Salem where he invested heavily in local real estate. That his wife was French, may explain the style of the house.

Only a story and a half high, it has such an imperious demeanor that it seems much larger. If it were a frame house one might be tempted to call it a cottage. But its brick construction gives it a distinct sense of monumentality. And its facade, organized as it is around a central bay and haughty tower, has the formality of a mansion.

An abundance of ornamental detail also fosters an impression of elegance. A freestanding portico with elaborate posts and lintels fronts the house. Bracketed cornices mark the roof lines. The patterned tile roof has dormers with gable-cap surrounds, and the tower has circular windows with semicircular hoods. The first story windows are headed with splayed bricks that form segmental arches. And on the side of the house is an unusual Graham gable (in essence a mansard roof in cross section) that simultaneously echoes the lines of the tower and contrasts with the flared curve of the main roof.

Still a private residence, the Evans House is listed on the National Register of Historic Places. But who designed it seems to have been lost to history.

GREGORY HOUSE,
THE QUEEN VICTORIA
1882: Cape May, New Jersey

This classic example of Second Empire styling was built for Douglas Gregory, who piloted steamboats on the run from Philadelphia to Cape May. It was built on the site of the old Columbia Hotel, which had burned to the ground in 1878 along with several other structures in town. It is recorded that the lot cost $3500 and the house another $4000, but neither architect nor builder have been identified.

True to the architectural conservatism of Cape May, the Gregory House adopted the French Second Empire style which by the 1880s had become definitely passe. Still, it was one of the more elaborate homes to rise phoenix-like from the ashes of the fire, and it displays some delightfully fussy features.

The curved mansard lends it a distinguished air, and the semioctagonal bays at the sides of the house create interesting complications in the facade and roof line. The house also combines a roomy American porch with the roof dormers, cornice brackets, and segmental-arched windows that were obligatory for houses in the French style. The bays, wings, and extended porches to the rear of the structure belie the formality of the presentational front.

Gregory sold the house in 1889, and it passed through a succession of hands until it became a summer boarding house early in the twentieth century. Today it is in use as a bed & breakfast inn called *The Queen Victoria*.

G.H. MEYERS HOUSE

1874: Bethlehem, Pennsylvania

Like his father-in-law, Francis Weiss (p. 91), George H. Meyers (1843-1912) made his fortune in anthracite. After studies at a seminary and a business college, he took over his father's mining interests and moved to Bethlehem where he married Carolyn Weiss and made prudent investments in prudent enterprises—banks and real estate among them. He is supposed also to have held interests in a zinc foundry, which may account for the cast-zinc ornament on the front of his brick Second Empire mansion, now an apartment building.

Built only four years after its next-door neighbor, the Meyers House illustrates the asymmetry and irregularity that quickly overcame the formal French Second Empire style in the United States. Like the Weiss house, it is dominated by a central block and tower, but here a pair of bay windows, one large, one smaller, have turned a plain facade into an undulating surface. Meanwhile, the main body of the house has broken into bays and wings, and the mansards have acquired graceful curves.

As with the Weiss house, a large lot allowed Meyers to set his residence well back from the street, something new for democratic Bethlehem where until the 1870s most houses had been built practically on the sidewalk. This physical distancing mirrored the social and economic schisms that were growing wider in post-Civil-War America.

Though the panic of 1873 flattened the market for houses of this sort to some extent, versions of them continued to be built here and there for a decade or so after the debacle. And long after the style per se had passed out of fashion, the imperious mansard roof was employed to lend a touch of elegance to the outsized homes of small-town gentry. For the very rich, the Chateauesque style upheld the French look as the ultimate symbol of success.

IRWIN HOUSE

c. 1872: Rochester, New York

One of a number of restored Victorian residences in Rochester's Corn Hill district, this house represents the Second Empire style, which became widely popular in the United States after the Civil War. The straight-sided mansard roof is the distinguishing feature of the style, but the modillions beneath the cornice, which are smaller and lighter than Italianate brackets, are also of French extraction.

Seen from the front, the residence might be taken for a town house, the impressive corner tower notwithstanding. A side view, however, gives a better idea of the scale of the structure. Its basic construction material is brick, but the window crowns, porches, and portico are of wood. The foundation is stone; the roof, slate.

Built as a three-family residence, the house originally belonged to Jacob S. Irwin, a file manufacturer. It remained in his family's possession until the 1950s when it was converted into apartments. In 1968 the house was acquired by the Genessee Landmarks Foundation and has since been refurbished by new owners.

HARRY PACKER MANSION
1874: Jim Thorpe, Pennsylvania

Renamed in the 1950s for a famous Olympic athlete, Jim Thorpe, Pennsylvania, was originally Mauch Chunk—an Indian name that means "Bear Mountain." Anthracite coal had been discovered in the Poconos as early as the 1790s, and within forty years it was being run down the mountainside on the celebrated "Switchback" gravity railroad to Mauch Chunk, where it was loaded into barges and mule-hauled down to Easton and Philadelphia via the Lehigh and Delaware Canals.

Asa Packer, who arrived in town in 1833, built the Lehigh Valley Railroad which supplanted the canals as a way of getting the coal to market. In the process he became quite wealthy, began contributing to various charities, and in 1860 built himself an Italianate mansion which still surveys the town from atop Packer Hill. A few years later he built the house shown here as a wedding gift for his son, Harold Eldred, better known as Harry.

Built in the fashionable French Second Empire style, it was designed by Addison Hutton, who is known as "The Quaker Architect." Hutton (1834-1916) had formed a brief partnership with Samuel Sloan in the late 1860s, and he later worked in Bethlehem where he designed the Packer Memorial Chapel at Lehigh University.

The house is constructed of brick and local stone with some cast-iron details. The corner tower was added to the existing structure in 1881 along with the arcaded porch of New England grey sandstone. The latter contains some fine carving, and the interior trappings include hand painted ceilings, carved mahogany paneling, marbles, etched glass, and period antiques.

Asa Packer died in 1879, and his son Harry followed him a few years later. He had contracted a fatal kidney disease and died at the young age of thirty-four. The house was sold at public auction in 1912 and has passed through a number of hands since then. Its most recent owners, the Handwerks, have been working to restore it to its original condition. Currently a bed & breakfast inn, The Harry Packer Mansion is one of several structures in the Old Mauch Chunk Historical District that are available for public tours.

103

GEORGE LITTLE HOUSE

c. 1875: Kennebunk, Maine

According to *Knickerbocker's History of New York*, one characteristic that differentiates the stolid Dutchman from the feckless Yankee is the latter's propensity for migration. "His first thought, on coming to years of manhood," wrote Washington Irving, "is to *settle* himself in the world,—which means nothing more nor less than to begin his rambles."

George Little, a Kennebunk native, seems to have done his share of rambling, but eventually he returned home to build the house shown here. The youngest of five children, Little (1820-1900) had seen his older brother Charles ramble down to Boston to found the publishing house of Little, Brown and Company; and when his own turn came, he too hit the road. It led ultimately to Fort Wayne, Indiana, where he listed himself in the city directory as "Produce Forwarding and Commission Merchant," and—according to E.E. Bourne's *History of Wells and Kennebunk*—conducted an "extensive and profitable business." Somewhere along the line he also obtained plans for a retirement home from an architect named George Trenham.

Trenham, another rambler, was from Leeds, England but immigrated to the United States and Fort Wayne, where he practiced first carpentry, then architecture. He is credited with designing the Allen County, Indiana Jail (since demolished) as well as a number of Italianate residences, some of which are still standing.

In 1874 Little returned to Kennebunk, where a year later he bought the land for his elegant French-inspired residence. Except that it is oddly placed on an expansive extraurban lot, the house would be a perfect example of a mansardic town house. It has the tall, narrow proportions required for building in the city and the same three-bay arrangement of doors and windows that was most commonly seen in row and town houses.

It also displays most of the features associated with Americanized versions of the Second Empire style. These include the curved mansard roofs with dormers and iron cresting, the brackets and modillions beneath the cornices, the rounded windows on the upper floors, and the off-center tower. The fancyworked braces on the porches and the elaborate wooden consoles that support the small balcony over the entry are also noteworthy. Recently restored, the house is still in use as a private residence.

WAGER HOUSE
c. 1875: Rhinebeck, New York

Also known as *Croff's Villa*, this house was built as the residence of
William Wager, a prominent citizen of the "charming and quiet Village of
Rhinebeck on the Hudson." It was designed by Gilbert Bostwick Croff, a
Saratoga Springs architect who published several pattern books during the
1870s. A drawing of the Wager house is included in his *Progressive American
Architecture*, a compilation of new and previously executed designs that was
issued by a New York publisher in 1875.

As the book serves to indicate, Croff's preferred style was the French
Second Empire. A majority of the houses contained in it display the same
mansardic elegance seen here. Generally they were two stories in height—not
counting the French roof—and almost invariably had a tower or some suggestion
of one. Evidently some of the finished products were quite large, for Croff
describes the Wager house as "small but beautiful."

Croff's books were apparently published in an attempt to appeal to
builders and contractors, but they were also probably intended as self
advertisements. It is not clear whether he was hoping to generate mail-order
business. But if he was, it is doubtful that he was able to generate the same
mass appeal that Palliser and Barber enjoyed a decade or so later. His designs
were too costly and elegant to be widely popular; and by the time his last book
was published, the haughty Second Empire was already beginning to be
superceded by more modern and egalitarian styles.

Figure 7: from *Progressive American Architecture*.

SPRAGUE HOUSE
1870: Ithaca, New York

This house in the French mansard style was built by Charles M. Titus, a businessman and speculator who developed an area of Ithaca called "The Flats," part of a large tract of land that had originally been set aside by the state of New York for Revolutionary War Veterans. The house was apparently built as a speculative project, for soon after it was completed, Titus sold it to his sister-in-law, Louisa, and her husband Joseph Brittin Sprague.

Sprague was a wealthy businessman who seems to have acquired his fortune in real estate. Besides a commercial block in Ithaca, he also had mining interests in Colorado and owned a farm in Ohio. When he acquired this house he had just returned from travels in Europe, Africa, and Madagascar. He was active in local politics, and though he was defeated in a bid for the state senate, he is remembered in Ithaca for his bold stand against the free grazing of cattle within the village limits.

No records have survived to show who designed and built the house, but it is interesting as an illustration of the new freedom that quickly overtook the formal Second Empire style in the post-Civil-War era. The symmetry that marked earlier representatives of the style has here given way to an irregular arrangement of flanking wings around an unusually tall, five-story tower. In recent years the former residence has been converted for use as an apartment building.

MANSARD-ROOFED HOUSE

1876: Saratoga Springs, New York

"At Newport life is public, if you will; at Saratoga it is absolutely common," wrote Henry James. "The difference, in a word, is the difference between a group of undiscriminating hotels and a series of organized houses."

He was right in a sense. Resort life at Saratoga Springs did center around several enormous and ostentatious hotels. On Broadway, the main thoroughfare through town, *The Grand Union* and its even more lavish rival, *The United States*, took up both sides of an entire block. But Saratoga also had its share of stylish and substantial houses, the summer places of seasonal visitors as well as the homes of permanent residents.

The house shown here, for example, originally belonged to Richard Southgate, who owned one of the lesser hotels in town, *The Long Beach*. Aristocrat that he was, James would probably have cited Southgate's house as another manifestation of what he called the "democratization of elegance." It was the French Second Empire, of course, but Americanized with clapboard siding, a homey front porch, and some applied decoration that suggests the influence of the Stick and Eastlake styles.

No information has survived to tell us who designed it, but in the good-story-anyway department is the tale that it was once the home of a New York State treasurer who secreted a large and as yet unrecovered sum of money somewhere inside. Today it serves as student housing during the winter and as a vacation home during the summer.

HECK-WYNNE HOUSE
c. 1875: Raleigh, North Carolina

This is one of three spec cottages built by Colonel Jonathan M. Heck in the early 1870s. Heck, it seems, had made a fortune manufacturing bayonets during the Civil War, and after the conflict he put most of his money in southern real estate. North Carolinians insist that he was not a carpetbagger, though some of them admit that he sometimes acted like one.

Arriving in Raleigh from West Virginia in 1871, Heck acquired twenty-five acres which he platted and subdivided into numbered lots. Planning his own residence—an impressive Second Empire mansion known today as the Heck-Andrews House—he engaged a New Jersey architect named G.S. Appleget. It is assumed that Appleget also designed the three cottages that Heck erected a couple of years later.

Though they were smaller and less formal than the Second Empire mansions of the rich, French cottages, as they were called, also derived a touch of elegance from the prominent and fashionable mansard roofs they wore. This example displays both convex and concave forms; and the roof of the tower strikes a particularly jaunty curve. Despite these refinements, however, the overall look is that of a homey cottage. In place of the portico that marks formal representatives of the style, the house has a comfortable porch that wraps around the base of the tower; and there has been no attempt to make it look as though it were built of anything but wood.

Evidently Heck's speculative venture paid off, for deed records show that he sold the houses to three different women in a two-day period in 1875. Like the Heck-Wynne house, the other two are still in use as private residences. Meanwhile, much of the land that was subdivided back in the 1870s has become the Oakwood Historic District, a neighborhood in which a number of other interesting nineteenth-century dwellings are preserved.

SEAVIEW COTTAGE

c. 1880s: Cape May, New Jersey

By the 1880s the mansard-roofed cottage had become a staple of vernacular architecture in the Northeast. Although the French roof had faded somewhat as a symbol of taste and distinction by that time, it was still an eminently practical and not unstylish way of adding usable attic space to a one- or two-story cottage. Houses in the French mode lost some of the hauteur they had previously possessed when they began to exchange such fussy details as modillions and keystoned window hoods for clapboard, extended porches, and other homey touches.

In many cities mansard cottages that have survived to the present are almost completely devoid of any sort of decoration. In Cape May and other parts of southern New Jersey, however, wooden gingerbread was *de rigueur* for almost every type of dwelling. Hence the fancy porch braces, brackets, and turned posts in *Seaview Cottage*, which was almost certainly built as a vacation house.

Ornamental dwellings like this one contributed greatly to the town's charm, but not everyone liked them. Writing in 1891, the editor of the *Ocean Wave* complained that ". . .the buildings in Cape May seem to have been designed by the architects of a half century ago. . .or by carpenters whose sole knowledge of architecture consisted of french (sic) roofs and gingerbread products of the scroll saw."

PARROT-CAMP-SOUCY HOUSE
c. 1885: Newnan, Georgia

In 1842, William P. Nemmons, one of the first white settlers in Coweta County, southwest of Atlanta, built the house that eventually blossomed into the mansard-roofed extravaganza shown here. Originally a two-story Greek Revival structure, it was extensively remodeled in the mid-1880s after it was acquired by John S. Bigby, a prominent judge in Newnan.

When Bigby's daughter, Callie, announced her engagement to Charles Parrot of distant Cartersville, the judge feared losing her to another town and promised her the house as a wedding present. To further strengthen the tie that binds, he founded the Newnan National Bank and appointed his new son-in-law president.

In 1885-86 the newlyweds spent more than ten thousand dollars remodeling and refurbishing the house in a High Victorian approximation of the French Second Empire style. Besides the distinctive mansard roof and central tower, they added delicate French bracketing, some Stick style touches, and an extended, wraparound porch—a feature most commonly associated with the Queen Anne.

The house also wears a wealth of applied ornament, much of it cast zinc. The raised interlacement over the entryway is an exceptionally elaborate example of a device that seems to have been quite common in Georgia during the late Victorian period.

Over the next century the house passed through a succession of hands until it was finally purchased in the early 1980s by the Soucy family. At that time it had been vacant for several years and was a near wreck. The new owners had to cope with termites, a leaky roof, hundred-year-old wiring, not to mention inoperable plumbing and heating.

Nonetheless, within two years of the purchase, they had completely restored the house in accordance with National Park Service guidelines. For their efforts they received an award from the Georgia Trust for Historic Preservation. The house is now listed on the National Register of Historic Places and serves as a private residence.

HALL PLACE ROWHOUSES

c. 1859: Albany, New York

Founded as Beverswyck by Dutch traders in 1624, Albany developed largely independent of the quasi-medieval patroon system that dominated most of the rest of New York until the Revolution. By 1750 it had developed as an important trading center, but its population remained small throughout the eighteenth century. After 1800, however, the advent of the steamboat and the opening of the Erie Canal spurred rapid growth. By 1820 Albany's population was still only about 13,000, but by 1840 it had risen to more than 33,000, and by 1850 it was nearly 50,000.

One visible effect of this rapid growth was the increased number of rowhouses that sprang up in the period before the Civil War. As late as 1840 detached houses were common in the city, but from 1845 until the turn of the century rowhouses predominated. Today, block upon block of attached houses in a variety of Victorian styles are preserved in Albany's several historic districts.

The examples shown here date from the late 1850s and are part of the Ten Broek neighborhood, which contains nearly a hundred nineteenth-century residences. Located just north of the original downtown area, it was developed for residential use between 1845 and 1875 and became home to a number of local lumber barons and nouveau-riche industrialists.

Unfortunately, the neighborhood centered around the site of an old Dutch cemetery that the local patroon, Stephen Van Rensselaer, had established in 1764 for the residents of his manor. This necropolis was graded higher than street level, and to the dismay of new residents, the bones and coffins of the dead often surfaced after heavy rains. Eventually the graveyard was relocated, largely due to the efforts of a landscape gardener, Joseph Hall, for whom Hall Place is named.

The wooden latticework that enlivens the porches of some of the houses on this short street is a survival from the period when rowhouses themselves were built of wood. The ever-present threat of fire in nineteenth-century America compelled almost all cities, sooner or later, to adopt ordinances forbidding frame construction in attached housing. In Albany most new rowhouses were brick by the 1850s, but wooden trim of the type seen here lingered on until the onset of the Civil War. After that, when not eliminated altogether, it tended to be replaced in new construction by cast iron.

TIFFTS HOUSES

c. 1870s: Buffalo, New York

By the 1870s Allen Street was one of Buffalo's main thoroughfares, but it had started out as a cow path, the daily stamping ground of a herd that belonged to an early developer named Lewis Fallie Allen. An agent of the Western Ensurance Company, Allen had arrived in Buffalo from Massachusetts in 1827, two years after the completion of the Erie Canal. Seeing opportunity in the making, he forsook the "ensurance" business for a more lucrative career in land speculation and began buying up real estate. Among the properties he acquired was a parcel of twenty-nine acres that eventually became the residential neighborhood known as Allentown.

Now designated as an Historic District, the area contains some of the city's oldest residences. Prominent among them are a row of houses that take up an entire block on Allen Street. They were built as a speculative housing project by William Tiffts, a well-to-do developer who had made his fortune in the grain business. Three of the original seven have been converted for commercial use, but the four seen here still serve as residences.

As indicated by differences in roof pitch and ornamental details, the houses were built in stages, a few years apart. The two at right are thought to have been constructed in 1870; those on the left, about 1878. Judging by style alone, however, they could have been built a decade or so earlier.

The Tiffts Houses represent the Italianate rowhouse in a very basic form. Although detached, they display the same uniformity, end-gabled street orientation, and three-bay facade arrangement that characterized row and town houses throughout the nineteenth century. Their Italianate features include asymmetrically placed doorways, carved scroll-and-pendant eaves brackets, and two types of windows—round headed and segmental arched. The pitch of the roofs is steeper than one might expect in Italianate houses, but given Buffalo's average annual snowfall, this deviation from the norm was probably a prudent one.

The older two of the four houses show some evidences of remodeling. The fanlights above the doorways are neo-Georgian additions; and the discoloration of some of the bricks marks the passing of wooden porches and balconies that seem to have been added to the facades around the turn of the century.

ITALIANATE HOUSE
c. 1878: Buffalo, New York

This frame house in Buffalo's Allentown district has the same tall proportions, street-wise orientation, and three-fold facade arrangement seen in the Tiffts houses (p. 121). Unlike those brick examples, however, this wooden one displays door and window ornament derived from formal Renaissance models. The elaborate surrounds take the form of segmental-arched hoods supported on thin colonnettes and capped with triangular pediments incised with delicate patterning.

Modest Italianate houses with high-style touches of this sort were common in the nearer suburbs of many mid-nineteenth-century cities. As the century progressed and cities expanded, however, they tended to be replaced in new construction by brick rowhouses in which some of the same ornamental details can be seen. This particular house originally belonged to one Susan C. Holland who apparently owned several other properties in Allentown.

CLINTON AVENUE ROWHOUSES
1873: Albany, New York

By the end of the Civil War, Albany had attained a population of 60,000 and was expanding away from its original site on the banks of the Hudson. The introduction of a horsecar line alone Clinton Avenue (formerly Patroon Street) helped create a new residential neighborhood north and west of the central downtown area. This district was soon dominated by rowhouses, many of which were erected by small-time building speculators who hoped to fill them with middle-class families in need of housing.

All went well until the 1920s when the area began to decline. The downturn accelerated during the Depression and continued throughout the postwar era as the automobile encouraged the development of new suburban neighborhoods far removed from the city. By the 1960s the Clinton Avenue area had become a virulent slum afflicted with all the problems associated with physical deterioration, declining property values, absentee landlords, and white flight.

In recent years, however, the creation of the Clinton Avenue Historic District has helped turn the neighborhood around. Restoration projects—both public and private—have made the district more livable, and many of the houses have once again become attractive to the middle-class families for whom they were originally built.

The row of newly renovated houses pictured here is thought to have been erected by a carpenter-builder named William Redden. Collectively they exemplify a house type—the flat-front Italianate rowhouse—that was common in Albany and many other Eastern cities in the period from the 1850s to the 1870s.

Generally such houses rose two to four stories above a raised basement and had a narrow front, which was divided into three parts. This arrangement allowed for two windows and an off-center entry on the ground floor and three corresponding windows on the upper stories. The high stoop with a service entrance below was especially characteristic of New York rowhouses. The word comes from the Dutch *stoep*, and the structure itself is thought to be a survival from the Netherlands, where precautions against high water were taken as a matter of course.

Among rowhouses it is usually only the ornamental details that distinguish one style from another. The same three-bay facade arrangement seen here was common from the Federal to the late Victorian period. What make the houses in this group *Italianate* are their bracketed cornices and decorative, segmental-arched lintels. The cornices, incidentally, are of wood, but the door and window surrounds are cast iron and were probably produced locally.

ORIEL-FRONT ROWHOUSE
1870: Albany, New York

When space and zoning laws allowed, bay windows and balconies were often added to flat-front rowhouses. These extensions enhanced the visual presence of the facade and also provided additional light, space, and air, all of which were at a premium in houses that shared party walls with their neighbors.

A typical bay-front arrangement was one in which a two- or three-story bay window replaced the paired windows of the flat-front rowhouse—an arrangement illustrated in the Saratoga Springs houses shown on p. 129. In Albany, however, a second-story bay window— or oriel—placed above the entry was a more frequently employed device for enlivening the facades of row and town houses. This characteristic feature of the city's architecture can be seen in this house in Albany's Center Square/ Hudson-Park Historic District. Except for the oriel, it follows the same essential plan and facade arrangement as the Clinton Avenue rowhouses shown opposite. The sills, lintels, and cornice brackets in this example, however, are all of wood.

MOUNT VERNON PLACE ROWHOUSES

c. 1862: Baltimore, Maryland

Extending in a great belt from Connecticut to New Jersey are vast deposits of a distinct type of sandstone that was laid down as sediment during the triassic period, 200 million years ago. Salmon pink when freshly quarried, it is nevertheless known as brownstone because it soon oxidizes to dusky hues that range from beige to chocolate. In the first half of the nineteenth century it was considered, at best, a cheap and inexpensive substitute for marble and limestone; but in the late 1840s it began to become fashionable.

The turning point came when Manhattan Episcopalians overruled architect Richard Upjohn and dressed Trinity Church, their new Gothic Revival flagship, with the appropriately dark and somber stone. When, not long afterwards, the same material appeared as the outer skin of several Fifth Avenue mansions, its future was assured. By the beginning of the Civil War, it had become *de rigueur* as a facing for all but the humblest dwellings in New York; and by the end of the century it was so closely associated with attached houses in the city that any sort of rowhouse, even a plain brick one, could correctly be called a "brownstone."

Brownstones may have achieved their greatest vogue in Gotham, but they were not unknown in other cities—particularly those with good water links to the quarries. They were quite popular in Albany, Boston, and Hoboken, less so in Philadelphia, and relatively rare elsewhere. In Baltimore brick rowhouses were ubiquitous, but brownstone fronts were uncommon, and few examples have survived to the present.

The exceptional houses shown here were probably built with the carriage trade in mind. They are thought to have been developed by a Colonel Richard E. France, who was apparently a speculative builder. He is supposed to have constructed and sold the entire row of six houses within a year of buying the empty lots in 1862. If he was gambling on making a quick killing, this up-to-date block may have helped tip the odds in his favor. With their Italianate brackets and window hoods, high stoops, and brownstone fronts, these houses would have been fashionable on almost any street in New York in the early 1860s.

BROWNSTONE ROWHOUSES
c. 1870: Brooklyn, New York

Today individual brownstones can be found in many parts of New York City, but entire rows of them in good repair are rarities. Not surprisingly, some of the best have managed to survive in Brooklyn where residential neighborhoods attractive to New York businessmen sprang up in the last half of the nineteenth century and where later development was less intense than in Manhattan.

The block of brownstones shown here is located in the Fort Greene section of town, east of Brooklyn Heights. Until midcentury, the area on which the neighborhood developed was rolling farmland, part of the Jackson Homestead which overlooked the East River. Soon after it was first developed in 1849, suburban cottages and villas began to appear. But by the early 1870s—when these houses on South Portland Avenue were completed—the neighborhood had taken on an almost completely urban character. Today the street is one of the few in the city that is still lined on both sides with uninterrupted rows of essentially intact brownstones.

As indicated by slight differences in the color of the facades, the individual houses were probably built in stages, a few at a time by a succession of builders. The older houses, which date from the late 1860s, are nominally Italianate; those from the 1870s, French. But the only obvious differences between them are the mansard roofs that cap the latter: the decorative details are consistent with either style.

CLINTON PLACE ROWHOUSES

c. 1884: Saratoga Springs, New York

This group of five attached houses in Saratoga Springs illustrates the standard bay-front house that evolved from the flat front. Its essentials include a large, full-height bay window and a small freestanding portico to shelter the entry. Houses like these were most popular in San Francisco and can be found elsewhere in small cities. In larger ones, flat-front rowhouses were more common.

These Saratoga examples also differ from their inner-city cousins in their proportions. With their generous width and abbreviated depth they are too boxy for most city lots—and too short: not counting the mansards, they are only two stories high. In Baltimore, Boston, New York, and Philadelphia by contrast three- and four-story rowhouses were more common.

Some modish Second Empire embellishments suggest that this group was designed to appeal to Saratoga's stylish and style-conscious inhabitants. Beneath the cornices, French modillions have replaced the heavy Italianate brackets of an earlier era; and below these are rows of dentils which recapitulate the same patterning. The houses also have rather fancy window hoods and distinctive mansard roofs, two of which are subtly inset and slightly lower than the others—a device which keeps the roof line from becoming too uniform.

Any thought that these houses were built for workers is quickly dispelled by a look at the available records. City directories indicate that during their first thirty years they were occupied primarily by middle-class professionals including a doctor, a lawyer, a Methodist Episcopal Minister, a diamond broker, and the owner and editor of one of the local newspapers. During the twentieth century, however, the apartments were increasingly tenanted by the likes of auto mechanics, dress makers, and beauty-shop operators and seem to have become somewhat *declasse*. By the 1960s many of the units had gone completely vacant, and the block languished a decade or so while waiting for new owners to restore it to a semblance of its original glory.

No information on who originally developed the complex has yet surfaced; but it is safe to assume that, like rowhouses elsewhere, these were built with the idea of maximizing ground space—which is to say, rents. In larger cities, this was standard practice, but in a small, relatively uncongested, and essentially horizontal town like Saratoga, it is remarkable. The appearance of rowhouses in such a setting indicates how firmly the European tradition of attached housing had taken hold on the East Coast.

J.P. SMITH HOUSE
1883: Providence, Rhode Island

Like the Arnold residence (p. 134), this two-family Second Empire town house is sited on the Dexter Parade, which was the focus of a prime residential district in 1880s Providence. It illustrates a bay-front facade arrangement already seen in Saratoga Springs (p. 129). Here a two-story bay on one side of the facade is balanced by a small portico and balcony on the other. The mansard roof is of patterned slate and has two gabled dormers. There are also modillions beneath the brackets and iron cresting on the balconies. Recently restored, the house originally belonged to John P. Smith, an employee of the Bank of North America.

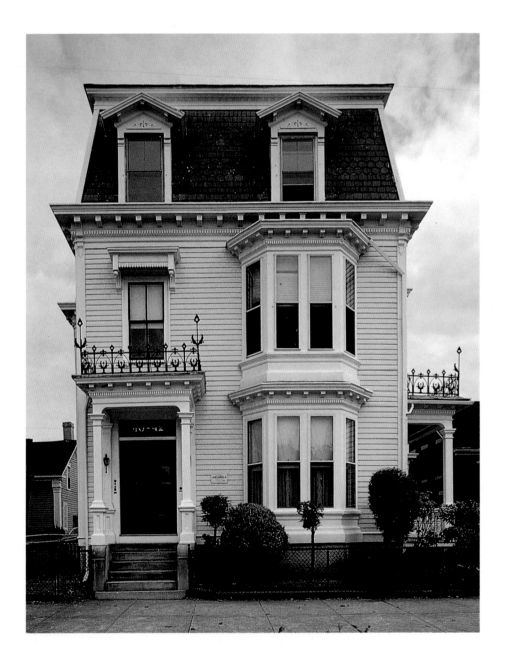

IDA SCHOOLCRAFT HOUSE

c. 1875: Richmond, Virginia

Though sometimes called the General Grant style, the French Second Empire had adherents even in the South. The former Schoolcraft residence in Richmond exemplifies the mansardic town houses that began to appear in most larger cities on the East Coast after the Civil War. Like the town houses of other periods, those in the French mode were generally built on a long, narrow plan with an asymmetric, three-bay front.

In this example the entrance third of the facade projects a few feet forward to create a narrow vestibule at the doorway. Though this extension stops short of becoming a full-blown wing, it nevertheless serves to produce irregularity in the facade and picturesque complications in the roof line.

Sometime in the recent past the house was converted for use as an office building and was refurbished in the process. The balustrade over the balcony is a reconstruction of a railing that was removed in years past: the other details, however, seem to be original.

Features typical of the Second Empire include the curved mansard roof—here shingled with patterned slate—and the tall, narrow, segmental-arched windows with their elaborate keystoned hoods. The full, classical arch of the entry is echoed in the stilted arches of the roof dormers and in the bay window at the side of the house. The placement of the latter, by the way, suggests that when the house was built, its neighborhood had a more suburban character than it does today.

DOUBLE HOUSES

c. 1880s: Pittsburgh, Pennsylvania

Though far removed from the coast, Pittsburgh has links with the established culture of the Atlantic that date back to prerevolutionary times. The town was founded mainly as a result of Anglo-French rivalry in the upper Ohio Valley. When the French established an outpost beyond the Alleghenies in what is now western Pennsylvania, the English followed suit and dispatched a young colonial major named George Washington to build a fort at the confluence of the Allegheny and Monongahela Rivers—the source of the Ohio. In 1758, with the French on the run, the settlement was duly named for the British statesman, William Pitt, who had had the good sense to stay home during the entire fracas.

For the next two hundred years the seams of bituminous coal that encircled Pittsburgh were the foundations of its prosperity. Local coal-based industries were abrew as early as 1790; and in 1818 an English traveler noted with satisfaction the hazy pall that hung over the town and predicted a bright industrial future for Pittsburgh. His augury proved correct, but by the time this row of semidetached houses were being built in the 1880s, visitors and residents alike were not as disposed to look with fondness on the soot and coal dust that were by then fouling the air in earnest.

Though the nine double houses shown here all follow the same plan, they were built in stages, the first of which occurred around 1882. The shared porches indicate that—unlike the Clinton Place Rowhouses in Saratoga Springs (p. 129)—they were built with the working man in mind. Still, they seem roomy enough and display some stylish flourishes: fancyworked porch details, segmental-arched windows, incised design work, ornately carved cornice brackets, and roof dormers. The roofs themselves achieve a Second Empire effect by means of a dodge often seen in rowhouses. The characteristic mansard slope appears at the front of each house, but on the sides, the walls drop to ground level without departing from the vertical.

By the 1960s these houses were so badly in need of repair that they were in danger of being razed altogether. This threat spurred the formation of the Allegheny County Landmarks Foundation which subsequently became a force in saving other historical structures in the city. Today Pittsburgh's several well-maintained historical districts reflect the community involvement, enlightened civic policies, and tough pollution-control measures that have helped transform the once gritty industrial town into one of the most livable cities in the United States.

B.F. ARNOLD HOUSE
1883: Providence, Rhode Island

In the first half of the nineteenth century, Providence's West End was still largely rural, but after the Civil War the installation of streetcar lines spurred its development as a residential neighborhood. Back in the 1820s an early resident, Ebenezer Knight Dexter, had left a parcel of land to the city for use as a military training ground. This eventually became the Dexter Parade, a ten-acre mall around which some of the more sumptuous late-nineteenth-century residences in the district were built.

One of them, the house pictured here, originally belonged to Benjamin F. Arnold, a partner in a grocery business. It is a type of house that is sometimes called a "Boston Duplex"—a two-family dwelling in which the second story is an independent unit, and the first and third floors are connected by stairways. This arrangement gave the landlord the advantages of both the ground and upper levels while leaving a second-story apartment for a tenant who, like as not, ended up paying for all three.

As evidenced by the robust semioctagonal turret, the house has definite leanings toward the Queen Anne, but there are also some carry-overs from the Stick style. On the turret, the vertical corner boards are belted with horizontal laths; and beneath the second-story windows are stylized braces and decorative panels, the latter newly painted to show the details. This sensitive restoration work recently won the house an award from the Providence Preservation Society.

134

A.B. GARDINER HOUSE

c. 1886: Providence, Rhode Island

Another type of city dwelling is illustrated in this three-family house. It is one of a pair that was built as income property for Aldrich B. Gardiner, a jewelry manufacturer. In 1892 his tenants included the widow of a jeweler, a bank cashier, a gas company clerk, a hardware store owner, an artist, and a gold pen and pencil case manufacturer.

The house, which combines Queen Anne and mansardic features, is perhaps typical of the multiple-family dwellings that were built in the Elmwood section of Providence in the last quarter of the nineteenth century. Originally a rural area on the outskirts of town, it had been subdivided by the 1850s but was slow to develop. One of the landowners, Joseph Jesse Cooke whose residence, *Elmwood*, gave its name to the entire district, succeeded in enforcing a policy of conditional land deeds that specified minimum costs for houses erected in the area. His intent was to create a low-density, model suburb with tree-lined streets and gracious, middle-class homes. But the practical effect was to send builders to areas where less rigorous standards were in force.

After Cooke's death in the early 1880s, some of his requirements were eased, and development proceeded apace. Although many of the neighborhood's late Victorian homes have been destroyed, others, like the Gardiner house, have been restored as part of recent efforts to reclaim the neighborhood from the blight that had overtaken it by the middle of the twentieth century.

DOUBLE HOUSE

c. 1877: New Castle, Delaware

The Gothic style was most at home in the country, but it made occasional appearances in the city as well. Gothic rowhouses were never terribly popular, but another urban type, the bay-front double house, often assumed some of the trappings of the style.

The example shown here was built as the residence of contractor Acquila M. Hizar from the plans of a well-known Philadelphia architect. Hizar, who had been orphaned at an early age, grew up in Chester, Pennsylvania. He enlisted in the Army of the Potomac at the outbreak of the Civil War and by the end of the conflict had risen to the rank of captain. Shortly after Appomattox he moved with his bride to New Castle. There he established himself as a builder-contractor and over the years erected numerous residences and public buildings, several of which are still standing today.

When it was time to build a house of his own, he turned to the Philadelphia firm of Isaac H. Hobbs & Son for an appropriate design. Hobbs, who also designed Skene Manor (p. 161), had begun his career as a builder; but by 1859 he had listed himself as an architect, and he seems to have enjoyed quick success at his new vocation. That same year *Godey's Lady's Book* featured one of his house plans, and he was soon a regular contributor. By the early 1870s, when *Godey's* circulation was nearly half a million, Hobbs was supplying the magazine with a new design every month.

This constant exposure in one of the most popular journals of the day probably brought him a lot of mail requests for existing plans, as well as commissions for new ones. The Hizar house seems to have been one of the latter, since it does not appear either in *Godey's* or in *Hobbs' Architecture*—a compilation published in 1873 and again in 1876. Moreover, working drawings that have survived seem to indicate that they were prepared expressly for Hizar.

In any case, the sort of double-bay front seen here traces at least to midcentury and Gervase Wheeler's design for a "Plain Timber Cottage-Villa," a plan which Downing included in *The Architecture of Country Houses*. The facade arrangement does not seem to have been a popular one for single-family homes, but it was a natural one for double houses and duplexes, great numbers of which were built in the nearer suburbs of many large northeastern cities. Few of the survivors, however, are as stylish as this example.

Figure 8: from *The Architecture of Country Houses*.

ROWHOUSE,
MOUNT ROYAL TERRACE

c. 1886: Baltimore, Maryland

The name *Mount Royal* traces back to a 340-acre estate that an early settler, John Hansen, acquired on the outskirts of Baltimore around 1720. Much of his rolling farmland eventually became part of Druid Hill Park, but some of it was ultimately subdivided for residential use as the city and its rowhouses crept towards the countryside.

The house shown here illustrates another scheme for transcending the basic flat front that dominated attached houses on the East Coast. The narrow facade has been divided roughly in two—one half taken up by a spindly-legged portico; the other by a shallow one-story bay overtopped by a balcony. Different arrangements of some of the same elements can be seen in attached houses in Albany and Saratoga Springs (pp. 129, 125).

Despite the fancy street name, the block of houses to which this one belongs is not truly a terrace in the architectural sense of a rowhouse group unified by an overall design scheme. It seems, rather, to have grown up spontaneously, a few units at a time, and was probably the work of a number of builders. The row contains several distinct house plans and is unified mainly by a range of eclectic ornamental details typical of the late nineteenth century.

In this house, layered bricks and patterned tile work add texture to the wall surfaces in much the same way that stick patterning did in frame houses of the same period. The scroll-cut and lathe-turned fancywork is in the Eastlake tradition, the iron-crested mansard that shelters the balcony is from the Second Empire, and the basket-arched window on the projecting bay is characteristic of the Queen Anne style. Gabled roofs—the only features needed to complete this rowhouse approximation of the most popular suburban styles of the period—can be seen in some of the other houses on the block.

McMILLAN HOUSES

1892: Savannah, Georgia

This group of attached houses was built during a spate of reconstruction that took place in Savannah after a fire destroyed several blocks of residential buildings in the spring of 1892. A few months after the blaze, the *Savannah Morning News* reported that a permit to build five two-story brick houses had been issued to the McMillan brothers, local builder-speculators who were active in town in the 1890s.

Sharp dealers, the McMillans were able to fit five "houses" into three city lots by building them as a terrace—a rowhouse group designed as a unit. The conceit here is that several small houses have been disguised as a single large one.

The group is also interesting as a solution to the late-nineteenth-century dilemma of creating picturesque variety in a rowhouse context. By nature less amenable to city lots and uniform treatment than its predecessors, the Queen Anne style with its organic plans and variegated surfaces presented a problem to rowhouse builders. The notion of a row of identical Queen Anne Houses was, in fact, something of a contradiction in terms. Here the problem has been solved by unifying the entire group of houses behind a single, asymmetrically composed facade.

In addition, multicolored bricks have been used to create surface interest—horizontal bands, checkerwork and zigzag patterning. These are examples of permanent polychrome, a sort of decoration that had been championed by the influential English writer, John Ruskin. It was most often seen in large public buildings; its use in private homes was unusual, and it was rare indeed in attached houses.

J.H. HUTCHINSON HOUSE

1882: Philadelphia, Pennsylvania

This late-Victorian town house was built for James Howell Hutchinson (1834-1889), a distinguished Philadelphia physician who came from a line of doctors that traces back to Revolutionary times. His grandfather, in fact, served as George Washington's surgeon general. Hutchinson, a pathologist and acknowledged authority on typhus and typhoid fever, was on the staff at Pennsylvania Hospital and also served as the Vice President of the College of Physicians and Surgeons in Philadelphia.

The properly fancy residence he built himself is located in Philadelphia's Rittenhouse district, which was one of the most fashionable neighborhoods in town in the last half of the nineteenth century. By the early 1880s, when the house was constructed, the area was dominated by the stylish homes of some of Philadelphia's leading families, not to mention such nouveau-riche entrepreneurs as department-store king John Wanamaker.

Among the professionals who ministered to this uptown clientele was Theophilus Parson Chandler (1845-1928), a newly risen star in the firmament of Philadelphia architecture. Originally from Boston, he had graduated from Harvard and later studied design both in the United States and at the *Atelier Vaudremer* in Paris. In the late 1860s he opened an office in Boston but in 1870 relocated to the City of Brotherly Love. Like two earlier Philadelphia architects, Samuel Sloan and Isaac Hobbs, he was a regular contributor to *Godey's Lady's Book*, which began featuring his designs in the late 1870s. Later in his career he helped found the Department of Architecture at the University of Pennsylvania.

Chandler's design for the Hutchinson House is notable as a solution to the late-Victorian problem of imbuing city houses with picturesque diversity. A half dozen types of windows in various arrangements and a range of ornamental details in carved brownstone add variation to what reads at first glance as a symmetrical facade. The impression of symmetry returns, however, when some of these elements are considered independently. Chandler has managed a nice trick in making the house irregular, symmetrical, and beautifully balanced all at once.

LAURA A. JONES HOUSE

1892: Savannah, Georgia

Aside from the sketchy information contained in a few newspaper items and assessor's records, almost nothing is known about the history of this house or of its early residents. Like the McMillan Houses (p. 140), it was constructed during a flurry of rebuilding that took place shortly after a fire destroyed several blocks in one of Savannah's oldest residential districts. A month after the conflagration, in May 1892, a building permit for a two-story frame house was issued to a Laura A. Jones. Evidently her new residence was completed promptly, for the following year the property was assessed at five thousand dollars.

The evocative tower with its reverse-ogee, candlesnuffer cap—an unusual addition for a relatively narrow city house—shows that romance was not dead in 1890s Savannah. In addition, a range of eclectic details shows an attempt to blend elements of the Queen Anne with the older Gothic Revival style. Besides the varied surface textures—patterned shingles, thin clapboarding, turned posts and balusters, dentils, and jig-cut panels—the house also displays at least four different types of arches: lancet, Tudor, rounded, and "arrow point." Also worthy of note are the unusual triple-hung windows.

Still a private residence after nearly a century of service, the former Jones residence is one of several hundred antebellum and Victorian structures that are still standing on the streets General James Oglethorpe laid out in 1733. Most of them owe their continued existence to the Historic Savannah Foundation, an organization which was formed when new development threatened to destroy the city's oldest residential sections in the mid-1950s. Today, Savannah's old town section is one of the largest urban National Historic Districts in the country.

142

TOWN HOUSE
c. 1905: Baltimore, Maryland

This residence in Baltimore's Bolton Hill Historic District illustrates the classical turn that town and rowhouses took in the late nineteenth and early twentieth centuries. Credited to the Baltimore architect Charles M. Anderson, it contains just enough classical references to indicate that the romantic tide was ebbing.

In contrast to Victorian borrowings from Grecian and Roman forms, which were often slapdash and off-the-cuff, the half portico at the entry in this example contains all the elements one would expect to find in a proper classical order. In addition the gently rounded bow window has the graceful curve of a neoclassical rotunda. Despite the stylistic shift, however, the facade arrangement of the house has the same three-bay arrangement of door and windows that was basic to city houses throughout the nineteenth century.

LOCKWOOD-MATHEWS MANSION
1869: Norwalk, Connecticut

Built just a few years after the end of the Civil War, this lavish mansion foreshadowed many of the developments that overtook American architecture later in the century. It was built for LeGrand Lockwood (1820-1872), one of the first great successes and one of the first great casualties of speculative capitalism in the United States. He was the descendant of a New England family that had settled in Norwalk in the seventeenth century, but he made his fortune in New York City. Starting off as a clerk in a brokerage house at the age of eighteen, he enjoyed a steady rise on Wall Street that culminated in 1863 when he was elected President of the New York Stock Exchange. During the Civil War he made a fortune in stocks, greenbacks, and, especially, government bonds, which he sold abroad to help finance the war effort. Like his rival and occasional ally Commodore Vanderbilt, he also made a good deal of money in shipping and railroads; and like the Commodore's offspring he was not afraid to spend his money on architecture.

Indeed, he is said to have spent two million dollars on the fifty-room stone mansion he built in his home town. Though he already had a house on Fifth Avenue, his country seat—one of the first great expressions of the aesthetics of consumption that overtook American architecture in the late 1800s—was truly worthy of his first name.

Significantly, the man he chose to design it was European. Detlef Lienau (1818-1887), a Dane from Schleswig-Holstein, had been rigorously educated at technical schools in Berlin and Munich and had spent an additional five years at the Atelier of Henri Labrouste in Paris. Armed with these impressive credentials he disembarked in New York at the end of 1848 and immediately established a thriving practice. Within a few years of his arrival he had everything from warehouses and cottages, government buildings and mansions to his credit. And his first major city residence, the Hart M. Shiff house on Fifth Avenue, introduced the Second Empire style to New York City.

Lienau's work was noticeably European—elegant and a bit formal by comparison with that of his American, and even his British, colleagues. Such opulence became possible in the United States only after the Civil War had disrupted the gentle dreams of Jacksonian Democracy and prepared the way for the unprecedented accumulation of wealth that occurred in the late nineteenth century.

As Ellen Kramer has pointed out, the Lockwood Mansion was "a true precursor of the mansions of the gilded age." But it also anticipated the eclecticism that preoccupied American architecture in the late Victorian era. It combined mansard roofs with steep-pitched Gothic gables, towers, wraparound porches, and an extended, irregular plan that owed much to the Italianate villa style.

The house was constructed of locally quarried granite, but some of the rarer woods and marbles used inside were imported from Italy—along with woodcarvers and stonecutters who are said to have arrived on the same ship. The particularly sumptuous interiors—mostly the work of Leon Marcotte, Lienau's friend and former partner—contain exquisite woodwork, etched glass, and some of the finest frescoed walls and ceilings on this side of the Atlantic.

It was all too good to be true, of course. The house was completed just in time for Black Friday—September 24, 1869. The crash was so sudden that even some of the robber barons were caught off guard. Jim Fisk was ruined—at least temporarily—but Commodore Vanderbilt, having been forewarned, escaped with his fortune intact. LeGrand Lockwood's firm was hard hit, and being a conscientious and scrupulous captain, he went down with his ship. Though he borrowed ten million dollars from Vanderbilt to cover his company's immediate debts, it wasn't enough, and he also had to mortgage his Norwalk mansion. When, two years later, Lockwood died of pneumonia, the Commodore foreclosed on his widow. Business, after all, was business.

In 1876 Charles Drelincourt Mathews, a New York importer, bought the estate for $90,000. It remained in his family's possession until the late 1930s, and in 1941 it was purchased by the City of Norwalk for use as a park. Portions of the grounds were soon whittled away to accommodate parking lots and part of Interstate 95, but when plans to raze the mansion were disclosed in the early 1960s, local citizens filed a successful suit to compel the city to honor the terms of the original purchase. In time a corporation was formed to ensure the continued existence of this prototypical mansion of the Gilded Age. It has since been declared a National Historic Landmark and is in use today as a house museum. Scrupulously restored and beautifully maintained, inside and out, it is open for tours by the public.

F.E. CHURCH HOUSE, *OLANA*
1870-72: Hudson, New York

Set on a great hill high above the Hudson, this exotic villa was originally the home and largely the creation of the painter Frederick Edwin Church. A member of the Hudson River School, Church (1826-1900) was one of the most successful American landscape artists of the nineteenth century. His talent, which began to manifest itself at an early age, was impressive even to his cautious and conservative parents who finally sent him to study with several accomplished teachers. His paintings of American landscapes brought him early success, and in search of more exotic subjects he soon embarked on a series of expeditions that took him to South America, the Arctic, and the West Indies.

It was an 1871 trip that inspired Church to build a villa-style house derived from Islamic models. Before taking his wife on a Continental tour which was to culminate in a visit to the Near East, Church commissioned Richard Morris Hunt to design a country residence in the Chauteauesque style. In Damascus, however, he found some of the mosques and other buildings so overwhelming that on returning home he dropped the French plan altogether and hired Calvert Vaux —A.J. Downing's former partner—to help him design a house based on what he had just seen.

Vaux's role seems to have been mostly that of a technical advisor. Church provided both the overall plan and the ornamental details that give the house its strong flavor of the Middle East. He was totally involved—some might say obsessed—with its construction, preparing more than three-hundred drawings while the house was being built.

In basic plan *Olana* is not far removed from the rambling, irregular compositions that marked the Italianate villas of previous decades. It is the stout square tower and the ornamental details that give the house a Persian look. The walls, constructed of site-quarried ashlar, are decorated with polychrome bricks and tiles to create an abstract mosaic, an effect echoed in the patterned-slate roof and in the voussoirs that trim the Islamic arches.

The initial construction was completed in 1872, and a studio wing was added in the early 1890s. Church, however, seems not to have made much use of this new addition. In 1877 an attack of inflammatory rheumatism left him unable to paint with his right hand. He learned to use his left for a brief spell, but after a time, it too began to ache, and he was obliged finally to give up painting altogether. He died in New York in the spring of 1900 shortly after returning from a winter in Mexico.

The house and grounds passed first to his heirs and later, in 1964, to the State of New York. Today *Olana*, loosely "Our Castle on High," is a state museum and park open to the public.

ARMOUR-STINER
OCTAGON HOUSE
1860-1872: Irvington, New York

In the 1850s and '60s a minor and somewhat cultish fad for octagonal-shaped houses swept the United States. At least one well-known architect, Samuel Sloan, tried his hand at the form and came up with *Longwood*, a memorable mansion that was constructed near Natchez, Mississippi in 1862. The most passionate advocate of the octagon house, however, was not an architect but a prolific publisher, pamphleteer, reformer, phrenologist, sexologist, and eccentric named Orson Squire Fowler.

With his brother, Lorenzo, and their partner Samuel Wells, Fowler published *The American Phrenological Journal, The Water Cure Journal*, the first two editions of Walt Whitman's *Leaves of Grass*, and a host of self-help books. A few titles should be enough to give their gist. There was *Vegetable Diet: as Sanctioned by Medical Men; Home Treatment for Sexual Abuses; Water-Cure Applied to Every Known Disease; The New Hydropathic Cookbook;* and *Parents Guide for the Transmission of the Desired Qualities to Offspring*.

Turning to architecture in 1848, Fowler published *A Home for All* under his own name. The case he made for octagonal houses was at once quasi-mystical and pseudoscientific. Noting that nature's forms were mostly spherical, and reasoning that the circle enclosed more space for its surface area than any other shape, he concluded that the nearly circular octagon was a far more natural, efficient, and economical form for houses than the traditional square or rectangle. To prove the hypothesis he built an octagon residence for himself in Fishkill, New York—*after* his book was released.

Though he sounds like a charlatan, there is no evidence to suggest that Fowler did not believe everything he wrote and advocated. And his motives were among the best. His principles were utopian, utilitarian, and (on the surface, at least) rational. He believed in democracy, progress, freedom of expression, free trade, equal rights for women, and the notion that health and happiness should be available to everyone. Perhaps the worst that can be said of him is that whenever he adopted a cause, legitimate scientists and thinkers began scurrying in the other direction.

For all the hocus-pocus, the Octagon idea wasn't half bad, and in recommending a basically circular form for houses Fowler was at least in good company: proponents of round buildings have included everyone from Vitruvius and Leonardo to Buckminster Fuller and Black Elk.

Though the Octagon fad was a limited one—estimates suggest that Fowler's book inspired only a thousand or two houses—it did produce some interesting structures. Probably the most lavish of them is the Armour-Stiner Octagon shown here. It was originally built in 1860 by Paul J. Armour, a banker and broker. But it was substantially remodeled and enlarged a dozen years later by Joseph Stiner, a wealthy tea merchant.

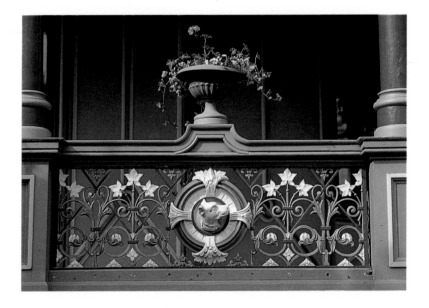

Ironically, considering Fowler's emphasis on utility and economy, the house that Stiner completed was essentially a huge *pavilion*—an ornamental structure, built as much to delight the eye as to satisfy any practical purpose. His additions included the extraordinary domed roof, the extended veranda that wraps around the entire house, and the eclectic decorative elements.

Stiner sold the house after his wife died in 1882. From the 1940s until 1976 it was the home of the writer and historian Carl Carmer. After his death it was acquired by the National Trust for Historic Preservation, which in turn sold it to the Joseph Pell Lombardis.

For over a decade, Lombardi, an architect who specializes in historic preservation, has been conducting a painstakingly accurate restoration of the house. Since he began, the roof has been restored with period slate, some missing details have been recast or re-carved, and the color scheme, inside and out, is as close to the original as microscopic and chemical analysis can make it. Though it serves today as a private residence, the house is available for group tours by appointment.

BATCHELLER MANSION

c. 1875: Saratoga Springs, New York

Although the springs at Saratoga had been known to the Indians of upstate New York from time immemorial, the Whites did not discover them until near the end of the eighteenth century. In 1771 a group of Mohawks carried Captain William Johnson, a hero of the French-Indian War, to the beneficent waters, which—he later testified—quickly healed his battle wounds. Pilgrims soon began arriving to test the springs' curative powers for themselves, and an inn was established at the site even before the Revolution broke out. By the early 1800s a small settlement had grown up, and locals were doing a thriving business catering to health-seeking visitors.

Gradually, however, Saratoga metamorphosed from a backwoods spa into one of the most fashionable and popular summer resorts of the Gilded Age. In the 1850s horseracing and gambling were introduced, and hotels of increasing lavishness were erected to house the growing throngs of summer visitors—the well-to-do of the nation.

Old money generally preferred Newport, as did Henry James, though he allowed that Saratoga was the more "characteristically democratic and American" of the two. "Democratic" hardly seems the right word, but the town did manifest a crude sort of equality in that everyone was rich—or at least seemed to be. Southern planters rubbed shoulders with northern industrialists and both mingled with midwestern coal and lumber barons. There were even a few lucky miners who had struck it rich in California and Nevada.

Though the hotels represented the heights of opulence, the town's domestic architecture also reflected the heady atmosphere at Saratoga. The houses ranged from the relatively modest homes of the local citizenry to the audacious mansions of wealthy summer visitors.

One of the most ebullient survivors from the period is the eclectic villa that George Sherman Batcheller built as a summer home. Batcheller (1837-1908) had been born in Batchellerville, a small town in Saratoga County. After graduating law at Harvard he began his long career in politics when he won election to the state assembly at the age of twenty-one. His political activities were interrupted by the Civil War, during which he attained the rank of lieutenant colonel; but after the conflict he resumed his law practice and returned to the assembly. In 1868 he was one of Grant's electors, and seven years later he was appointed to the International Tribunal for the Legal Administration of Egypt—a special court that adjudicated disputes between natives and foreigners. He also served in the Treasury Department and as a minister to Portugal under Benjamin Harrison. In 1898 he returned to the Tribunal at the request of the Egyptian Government.

Though built as a summer place, Batcheller's Saratoga mansion became his year-round residence after 1902. He called it *Kasr-el-Nouzia*—Arabic for "Palace of Pleasure"—though its design does not seem to have been significantly influenced by Middle Eastern sources. It is, however, quite eclectic, combining Italianate and classical touches with hints of Ruskin's favorite Venetian Gothic and just a suggestion—in the roofs and shaped gables—of the Chateauesque style that was to become popular with the very wealthy not many years hence.

The house is of frame construction and is clad with thin, vertical laths carefully matched and painted to resemble whitewashed stucco. The basic design has been credited to Batcheller himself, but the working plans were drawn up by the architects Charles Nichols and John Halcott. That the two were based in Albany may help to explain the similarity between the oriel windows seen here and those that grace many of the surviving rowhouses in their home town (see p. 125).

After Batcheller's death, the mansion changed hands a number of times. By the 1960s it was in use as a rooming house and had begun to fall into disrepair. It has since been restored by new owners and is once again in use as a private residence.

151

THREE-GABLED HOUSE

c. 1875: Bridgeton, New Jersey

Bridgeton, in the southwest corner of New Jersey, was settled by Quakers in the late 1600s and later prospered from farming, woolen mills, and small factories. Today it boasts more than 2200 surviving historical structures ranging from the Colonial to the late Victorian period. Among the latter are scores of basic houses that have been enlivened with the flat-cut gingerbread that seems to have been endemic in the southern part of the state.

Though it has a few idiosyncrasies of its own, the house shown here exemplifies a residential type that was very common in New Jersey in the last quarter of the nineteenth century. Its basic organization—a side-hall plan with central bay and gable—is similar to that of the Joseph Hall Cottage in Cape May (p. 155). The verticality of the facade along with the steep pitch of the roof gives it a Gothic flavor. But the house also has details associated with the Italianate—rounded windows, eaves brackets, and bay windows. The latter, however, are unusual in that they are two-sided and half-diamond in section. The portico with its round roof and fluted pillars is also quite individual.

JOSEPH HALL COTTAGE
c. 1870: Cape May, New Jersey

This example of Cape May Gothic was not a vacation cottage but the year-round residence of Joseph Hall, a wheelwright by trade. No architect has been definitely associated with its design, but it is thought to be the work of J. Stratton Ware, a local contractor who is known to have built several similar houses in town—including his own residence next door.

As illustrated here, houses of this type were built on a side-hall plan and had a central bay and gable flanked by two small dormers. Eaves returns and cornice brackets were also standard issue, and the porches were generally dressed with a Cape May specialty—flat-cut gingerbread.

In their essentials such houses were similar to Downingesque cottages but had a more vertical emphasis, rising a full two stories beneath a gabled rather than a hipped roof. For a better idea of these differences, compare this example with the H.M. Brooks house shown on p. 25.

Still a private residence, the Hall Cottage is one of a number of well-maintained Victorian homes on Cape May's Hughes Street. Its color scheme is correct, but reversed: it was once a blue house with *gold* trim. And it also has its original iron fencing—a rarity at the seashore, where the salt spray generally disposes of ferrous frills in a decade or two.

GEORGE P. LITTLE HOUSE
1868: Pembroke, New Hampshire

"The home of George P. Little, on Pembroke street, was erected in 1869, from the plans of George Williams, of New York. It has twice undergone remodeling and improvement, and is now one of the most desirable residences in the Merrimack valley. Attached to the house is a farm of 175 acres, which is one of the noted farms of the Merrimack valley, whose fertile intervales largely comprise the farmstead. Mr. Little, when a boy, lived upon this farm with his mother. The place was then the property of Judge Stevens heirs, and his boyhood resolutions for prosperity have led him in his manhood to become the possessor of his early home."

The quote is from a book of photographs, *New Hampshire Homes*, published in 1895 by James A. Wood of Concord. Other sources seem to think the house was constructed in 1868, but they agree in the other particulars. Little, who was born in 1834, left Pembroke at an early age, worked at several different occupations, and returned to town wealthy enough to buy his boyhood home and establish a farm. There he bred Jersey cattle and blooded horses. Meanwhile, Mrs. Little bore him seven children.

The house is a two-story, side-hall structure with a centered gable—the same basic scheme seen in the Hall Cottage in Cape May (p. 155). However in this example the gable is more decorative than functional and may have been one of the improvements mentioned by Wood. The house also combines Italianate brackets with Stick style elements—stylized trusses in the gable and curved braces on the porch. Judging from Wood's photograph, the facade seems to be much the same today as it was in 1895.

MARK TWAIN HOUSE
1874: Hartford, Connecticut

By the time he built this house, Samuel Clemens had started and abandoned a half dozen careers and had wandered a considerable portion of the globe. At the age of twelve he took a job as a printer's devil, and for the next quarter of a century he worked successively as a riverboat pilot, prospector, newspaperman, short-story writer, and professional lecturer. During those years he sternwheeled up and down the Mississippi and Ohio Rivers, rode a stagecoach west to Nevada, and sailed to Hawaii, Europe, and the Holy Land.

But in the early 1870s his bohemian ramblings came to an end when he married Olivia Langdon, a coal heiress from Elmira, New York. His new wife took pains to mend some of the unfortunate habits he had picked up along the way, and with the proceeds from his first book, *The Innocents Abroad*, he settled down to a life of genteel domesticity and literary fame in Hartford, Connecticut.

Of the house Twain built soon after his arrival in town, a local newspaper opined that it was "one of the oddest buildings ever designed for a dwelling." An overstatement, no doubt, but there is no denying its strangeness.

If it had been constructed in wood, it would be easy to identify as an example of the Stick style. The complicated polychrome brickwork, in which verticals and diagonals interrupt the horizontal courses, is analogous to the stick patterning seen in frame houses of the same period. The trusses and bracing in the gables and porches are also consistent with the style.

The house is credited to Edward Tuckerman Potter, an architect from Schenectady who had apprenticed with Richard Upjohn and is remembered chiefly for his ecclesiastical work. It seems apparent, however, that Twain himself exerted considerable influence on the design. Indeed, the house looks like some implausible riverboat run aground in the hills outside Hartford.

All told, Twain and his family occupied their curious dwelling for nearly twenty years, a period during which he wrote some of his best work and entertained some of the most interesting personalities of the Gilded Age—a term, incidentally, which he made popular.

In the 1890s, however, his good fortune began to wane. Bad investments forced him into bankruptcy, and while he was away on a lecture tour to make good on his debts, his favorite daughter, Susy, contracted spinal meningitis and died before he could reach home. After that, Twain records, he was himself somewhat leary of the house, and his wife flatly refused to set foot in it. The Clemenses took up residence elsewhere, though they retained the Hartford place until 1903.

Twain himself died in 1910, and for nearly two decades afterwards the fate of his former home remained uncertain as it passed from hand to hand, serving variously as a school for boys, an office building, and a warehouse. In 1929, however, the Friends of Hartford raised money to make it a permanent memorial to its original owner. It was subsequently declared a National Historic Landmark. Restored and refurbished with Twain memorabilia and other Victorian artifacts, it is open for public tours.

JUDGE POTTER HOUSE,
SKENE MANOR
1875: Whitehall, New York

Whitehall, in the Champlain Valley, was originally known as Skenesborough and might have retained the name had its founder picked the winning side during the Revolutionary War. As fate would have it, however, the British lost, Colonel Phillip Skene returned to England, and Skenesborough became Whitehall.

Skene Manor, the "quiet, unobtrusive" piece of architecture that now dominates the town, was designed by Isaac H. Hobbs, who in the 1870s succeeded Samuel Sloan as the reigning architect at *Godey's Lady's Book*. A drawing of the house appeared in the December 1876 issue of the magazine along with some comments by the architect that are worth quoting at length:

"The above building is in the Gothic style of architecture. It was built by Judge Potter, of the Supreme Court of New York, for a permanent residence upon the side of a high, rocky hill, overlooking the town of Whitehall, New York. It is situated on a level plot of ground, about one hundred and fifty feet above the town, with the hill rising high above it in the rear, and is one of those quiet, unobtrusive pieces of architecture that is seldom seen in this country. It was constructed of white sandstone, laid rubble, and pointed (sic) the color of the stone, with a black uniform line marking the joints. The roof is covered with slate; the porches, cornices, etc. are of wood. The house is very commodious, having all of the necessary apartments to make it a first class residence. It is considered by many of acknowledged taste to be one of the most successful and beautiful residences in the northern portion of the State, although in point of expense very many treble it in cost, which was about $25,000. The interior is well finished, good plumbing, heating, and all other conveniences of the present day are abundantly and richly supplied. The above drawing can give but a faint idea of its beauty, as the nice balance of parts and the due quantities of effect cannot be fully appreciated without viewing the building, surrounded by the scenery, with which it was organized to be associated."

Though Hobbs doesn't mention it, his plans were executed by a local builder named Almon C. Hopson. Originally called *Terrace Hall*, the house later became known as *Skene Manor*. Today it is listed on the National Register of Historic Places and serves as a bed & breakfast inn.

Figure 9: "Suburban Residence," from *Godey's Lady's Book*.

THUMBELINA COTTAGE
c. 1875: Chautauqua, New York

After the Civil War the old-fashioned religious camp meeting began to take on a more organized and stable form. Under the auspices of evangelical churches like the Baptists and Methodists, permanent summer resorts began to spring up, usually on the shores of a convenient ocean or lake. Ocean Grove in New Jersey, Pacific Grove in California, and Oak Bluffs on Martha's Vineyard were just three among scores of religious summer colonies that were established in the 1870s and '80s. Perhaps Robert Louis Stevenson summed up the atmosphere of these places when he perceived in Pacific Grove "a life of teetotalism, religion, and flirtation, which I am willing to think blameless and agreeable."

Probably the most famous of these summer communities was Chautauqua, which grew out of the Methodist-Episcopal camp meetings that were held on the shores of Lake Chautauqua in western New York. In 1874 two church members, John Heyl Vincent and Lewis Miller, proposed the formation of a program to train Sunday-school teachers, and this soon developed into a course of general adult education. Summer classes offering instruction in both religious and secular subjects were organized, and these were supplemented with lectures by authors, travelers, musicians, war heroes, and politicians.

As in other, similar resorts, the architecture that grew up in Chautauqua was geared to the needs of summer visitors and tended to be light, airy, rather ornamental, and a bit insubstantial. The diminutive house shown here has the same projecting roof as Ocean Grove's *Centennial Cottage* (p. 164), and a similar system of gable braces—a variation on the hammerbeam truss. The house was built in 1873 after the Reverend A.D. Norton of South Cleveland, Ohio obtained a ninety-nine-year lease on the lot. Today it is still in use as a private vacation cottage.

SUMMER HOUSE

c. 1883: Chautauqua, New York

A larger and more substantial but still highly ornamental summer cottage in Chautauqua is this house, which served for a time as the headquarters of The Woman's Christian Temperance Union. The style is quite individual but seems to be based on Gothic forms with a few Italianate touches thrown in for good measure. Roughly octagonal in plan, the house is dominated by a central front gable that shelters a second-story porch. To the rear is a tower-like wing that may have been an addition to the original structure. The outer cladding is composed of thin tongue-and-groove vertical boards *sans* battens.

CENTENNIAL COTTAGE

1874: Ocean Grove, New Jersey

Ocean Grove on the Jersey shore was founded as a vacation resort by the Camp Meeting Association in 1869. It was billed as "God's Square Mile of Health and Happiness," a place where the saved could enjoy fresh air and sunshine, just like the sinners who frequented Newport and Saratoga.

Baedeker's guide thought the place "curious enough to repay a short visit," but marveled that "thousands of persons, young and old, voluntarily elect to spend their summer vacations under a religious autocracy which is severe both in its positive and negative regulations." Smoking and drinking were taboo, of course, as was the theatre and bathing on Sunday; and attendance at daily prayer meetings was mandatory.

Still, the summer colony was popular with the righteous, and the tents that served the first visitors were soon replaced with scores of small vacation houses. In general these were light, airy structures built to suit the simplified needs of summer cottagers. The designs were so basic that they seldom required an architect, and most seem to have been planned as well as constructed by local builders.

A favorite type of summer house was a sort of seaside Chalet. As illustrated here, it took the form of a gabled box with the main roof extending out to shelter the upper level of a two-tiered porch. The posts, beams, and braces that supported this extension were exposed for all to see, and the trusswork was generally filled to overflowing with flat-cut gingerbread—echoes, some say, of the fancy fringes that decorated the original tents.

This particular example displays some interesting departures from the norm. The first floor is narrower than the second, thus making room for a side porch; but the facade still manages to convey the illusion of rigorous symmetry.

The house originally belonged to the family of Joseph Fels, the Philadelphia soap king of Fels Naphtha fame. But in the late 1960s it was donated to the Camp Meeting Association—just in time for Ocean Grove's centennial celebration. It has since become *Centennial Cottage* and is open to the public under the auspices of the Historical Society of Ocean Grove.

JOHNSON COTTAGE, *THE PINK HOUSE*

c. 1879: Cape May, New Jersey

Originally built for Eldridge Johnson, *The Pink House* is one of the most fancifully decorated of the vacation cottages still standing in Cape May. No architect has been associated with its design, but it is thought to be the work of Charles Shaw, the contractor who also built the Emlen Physick House (p. 171). Like the Gregory House (p. 97), this one was constructed after the great fire of 1878. It is a variation on the seaside chalets already seen in Ocean Grove and Chautauqua. Unlike those other examples, however, the upper porch in this house is sheltered by a roof of its own. Except for some minor details that have been repaired, the lacy scroll-cut openwork that covers the facade is part of the original construction. The house has been painted pink since about the turn of the century.

In 1960, *The Pink House* was scheduled to be destroyed in the wake of a hurricane that had buffeted, deluged, and left Cape May half buried in sand. Fortunately, however, the house was saved when concerned townsfolk arranged to have it moved several blocks to a new location. It was subsequently renovated and restored and is now in use in the summer months as a shop that deals in Victoriana.

HEART-BLOSSOMS-BY-THE-SEA

c. 1870s: Ocean Grove, New Jersey

This seaside cottage, which has provided backgrounds for everything from Woody Allen films to coffee commercials, is located on Ocean Pathway, which *National Geographic Magazine* once called "The most beautiful short street in America." It was built as the summer place of Joseph Billbrough, a Philadelphia lawyer who spent his vacations at the religious summer community in Ocean Grove. It is thought to have been built by John Doleson, a local carpenter, who may have designed it as well.

Like most of the houses on Ocean Pathway, this one typifies the seaside chalet style that was a staple of vacation architecture in the late nineteenth century. This example is perhaps a bit larger than *Centennial Cottage* (p. 164), another Ocean Grove house, but it has the same projecting roof, the same exposed trusses, and the same taste for carpenter's lace.

Though built as a summer cottage, the house is now in use as a full-year residence. The poetry was added by a recent owner, Mrs. Neil Chambers, who took it verbatim from an 1890 camp meeting report. The author's initials, "E.H.S.", are those of the Reverend Ellwood H. Stokes, who helped found the Ocean Grove Camp Meeting Association in 1869.

W.J. CLARK HOUSE, *VILLA VISTA*
1879-80: Branford, Connecticut

Originally the summer home of a Connecticut Yankee who made a small fortune in the hardware business, this intriguing house is one of the late works of the New Haven architect Henry Austin. In addition, it illustrates the nineteenth-century building mode that is now known as the Stick style.

This architectural mode embodied a sort of ornament that emphasized, even celebrated, wood-frame construction. Stick style houses made no attempt to simulate stone or brick. Indeed they took every opportunity to reveal the wooden skeletons that lay beneath their outer skins. In this and in some other respects the Stick style represented a mid-Victorian continuation of some of the concerns of the Gothic Revival. Contemporary architects, in fact, sometimes referred to the style as "Modern Gothic."

In the present example some hallmarks of the Stick style can be seen in the broad overhanging eaves, extended rafters, and decorative gable trusses, which—on the porch, at least—actually help support the roof. There is also a hint of the diagonal stick applique that literally covered more florid representatives of the style. Here the distinctive cross patterning makes only a single, subtle appearance high up on the square tower. Meanwhile, the steep pitch of the tower roof and the pointed arches of the two-tiered porch are clear echoes of the earlier Gothic Revival.

As seen elsewhere (pp. 162,164) the device of extending the main roof to cover the upper porch was quite common in small seaside chalets. But this example overlooking Long Island Sound is really more a villa than a cottage.

It first belonged to William Judson Clark, the son of a farmer from Southington, Connecticut. Born in 1825, Clark was educated at local schools and came of age in plenty of time to join the California gold rush of 1849. If he found paydirt, it is not recorded, but it is known that he was back in Southington by 1854. There, with his brothers, he founded a machine shop that manufactured those essentials of hardware—nuts and bolts. When the Civil War came, he marched off with the 20th Connecticut and by the end of the conflict he was a lieutenant. In the meantime, his plant had made him moderately wealthy producing hardware for the Union war effort.

According to an item in the *New Haven Journal and Courier* (August 5, 1880), Clark's summer house in Branford was designed by "Harry Austin, Esq." This, of course, was the same Henry Austin (1804-1891) who had designed the demolished but unforgettable New Haven Railroad station of 1848.

Austin's long career spanned more than half a century. At a young age he became a carpenter's apprentice and as a young man he worked for a time with the leading Greek Revivalist of the day, Ithiel Town. His employer's influence can be seen in some of the Greek Revival cottages Austin designed soon after he set up his own New Haven office in 1837. But his later work included many examples in the Italianate style, the most famous of which is the Morse-Libby Mansion in Portland, Maine (p. 79).

Austin's career peaked in the 1860s, and he was well into his seventies when he designed the Clark house, so the villa may be considered something of a swan song. In fine repair, it is listed on the National Register of Historic Places but remains a private residence.

EMLEN PHYSICK HOUSE
1878-79: Cape May, New Jersey

This exemplar of the Stick style was once the residence of Dr. Emlen Physick, Jr., grandson of Dr. Phillip Syng Physick, an eminent American surgeon. Originally built for his mother, the house and the rest of his grandfather's estate passed to the younger Physick on the condition that he carry on the family tradition by becoming a doctor. He did in fact graduate from medical school, but there is no evidence that he ever practiced anything more demanding than croquet. Eschewing the complications of patients and house calls, he seems to have pursued the life of a country gentleman in his overgrown cottage by the sea.

The construction of the house is credited to Charles Shaw, who was considered one of the most skillful carpenters active in Cape May during the late 1870s. And it is also generally accepted that it was designed by Frank Furness. Though there are no documents to confirm the attribution, the bold proportions and chunky solidarity of the Physick house are typical of his domestic work, and he is known to have designed an almost identical residence in the environs of Philadelphia.

One of the leading architects in that city in the late nineteenth century, Furness (1839-1912) was noted for his aggressive, some say ugly, designs. Though a minister's son, he failed to live up to any stereotypes that might be attached to that accident of birth and cultivated a personal style as bold as his architecture. During the Civil War he rose from private to captain and was awarded a Congressional Medal of Honor on the way up. He is remembered for wearing garish plaids, a red walrus mustache, and a permanent scowl. He was also said to have been a master of invective and seems to have been as hard on his clients as he was on his employees.

His house architecture reflects the influence of his teacher Richard Morris Hunt, who helped create the Stick style before moving on to indulge his passion for the Chateauesque. The Physick House displays several features typical of the earlier style: enormous braces on the porch; monumental roofs with steep inclines and jerkinhead dormers; and horizontal and vertical strips which frame the wall surfaces in stylized imitation of the skeletal posts and joints that actually support the structure.

As George E. Thomas has pointed out, the house is also interesting as perhaps the only one in Cape May that was at all fashionable when it was built. The rest of the town's architecture was resolutely conservative if not downright *retarditaire*.

Today the former residence is open for public tours under the auspices of the Mid-Atlantic Center for the Arts. The organization was formed in the late 1960s to save the Physick House from destruction, and it went on to help Cape May present itself as one of the premier bastions of Victoriana in the country. Today the town's Historic District comprises about six hundred well preserved structures from the late nineteenth and early twentieth centuries.

BORIGHT HOUSE, *GREY GABLES*

1890: Richford, Vermont

The Boright House is a straightforward copy of the Bridgeport, Connecticut residence of George Palliser (1848?-1903), the most famous of the nineteenth-century mail-order architects. He was not the first in his profession to employ the mails to do business, of course. Earlier architects—Alexander Jackson Davis, most notably—often dispatched stock plans to distant clients who requested them. Palliser's claim to fame is that he was the first to adopt a systematic approach to the concept of architecture by mail and the first to base a major portion of his business upon it.

An Englishman by birth, he arrived in the United States when he was twenty and began working as a carpenter in Newark, New Jersey. Several years later he relocated to Bridgeport, Connecticut, where he designed an entire subdivision of speculative suburban houses for the town's entrepreneurial mayor, P.T. Barnum. It was in this period that Palliser began to develop the idea of serving clients via the mails, and he shortly produced a slim paperback volume of plans which sold for only a quarter a copy. "With this booklet," wrote M.A. Tomlan, "the practice of mail order architecture was established."

Model Homes for the People (1876) contained forty-eight house designs in woodcut and listed the cost of plans and specifications for each. Readers were invited to choose a design they liked and to write the architect with a description of the site along with particulars about any special requirements they might have. Palliser would respond with sketches which—if they met with the client's approval—were to be followed by working drawings and specifications. All this was accomplished at a fraction of the cost of an architect's standard commission.

By 1878 Palliser had been joined by his younger brother Charles, and under the name Palliser & Palliser the two went on to produce more than twenty other publications over the next thirty years. Thousands of their houses were erected all over the United States, and the brothers claimed that some of their designs were executed as many as "twenty to fifty times by our certain knowledge." Despite this, they denied that they were in the ready-made-plan business and asserted that "we have not found two persons wanting to build the same house."

George Palliser seems to have been particularly proud of the design for his own Stick style-Queen Anne residence in Bridgeport. It appeared as the first plate in his *American Cottage Homes* (1878) and also on the cover. In scale and complexity, however, it was atypical of the run of houses that the firm designed.

The version of the design shown here was originally the home of Sheldon Boright, the proprietor of a dry goods store in the small town of Richford on the Canadian border. Local tradition has it that a few years before building

Figure 10: from Palliser's *American Cottage Homes.*

the house Boright planted several saplings which he named after his daughters. Later, when his new home was under construction, he used the filled-out trees to make several of the turned posts on the front balcony—thus, as it were, incorporating his family into the very structure of the dwelling. Today *Grey Gables*, as it is known, is being restored for use as a bed & breakfast inn.

173

M.L. PECK HOUSE
1881: Bristol, Connecticut

The house shown here is one of a number of substantial nineteenth-century residences that recall the era when Bristol was the center of the clockmaking industry in America. Like many of the others, it is located in the city's Federal Hill Historic District, which developed as a prime residential neighborhood in the last decades of the century. It originally belonged to Miles Lewis Peck, treasurer and, later, president of the Bristol Savings Bank; and it was designed by his brother Theodore, a Waterbury architect who is credited with several other notable residences and buildings in Bristol.

In style it displays some features commonly associated with the Queen Anne—hipped roof, varied surface textures, wraparound porch—but its vertical emphasis and some of its details indicate an evolution from earlier styles. The steep gables with their perforated bargeboards are survivals from the Gothic Revival, while the trusses, chamfered posts, and curved braces on the veranda are remnants of the Stick style. The color scheme is believed to be original to the house.

FREDERICK BUNNELL HOUSE

1888: New Haven, Connecticut

Whitney Avenue, a fashionable residential street in New Haven, came into its own in the last two decades of the nineteenth century. Once sewerage lines and horse-drawn trolley tracks were in place, development was swift, and the avenue was soon lined with new residences in a variety of styles and sizes. These ranged from substantial brick and masonry manses like the Chateauesque Burwell House (p. 222) to more modest frame cottages like the one pictured here.

Of its origins little is known except that it was first owned by Frederick Bunnell, who worked as a cashier at the New Haven Savings Bank during the 1890s. Neither architect nor builder has been identified, but the house might well be a stock design erected by a local contractor or house carpenter. It exemplifies a suburban dwelling type that arose in enormous numbers on the outskirts of almost every northeastern city during the late nineteenth century.

Its basic form is that of an L-shaped, hipped-roof cottage, enhanced by a few stylistic touches. The turned porch posts and spindles and the multiplicity of surface textures—patterned shingles, belt courses, clapboard panels—are all associated with the Queen Anne style. The color scheme, though not original to the house, is accurate for the period.

Houses of this type were quickly and economically constructed, but they were built at a time when carpenters still took pains with their work: those that haven't suffered complete destruction tend to age remarkably well. For much of the present century the Bunnell house was well cared for, but during the 1960s, when it was pressed into service as student housing, it was allowed to deteriorate badly. Ironically, what was nearly spoiled by Yalies and absentee landlords was put right by a group of inner-city youths in a summer jobs program. After they helped new owners restore the residence to its original bloom, some of them went on to apply their newly acquired skills in their own neighborhoods.

W.E. EMERY HOUSE, *ROSE LAWN*

c. 1874: Flemington, New Jersey

The country around Flemington, New Jersey was originally inhabited by the Lenni Lenape Indians, but by the middle of the eighteenth century it had been settled by Whites and cleared for agriculture. In 1756 Samuel Fleming purchased land in the area and opened a tavern which became the nucleus of the village. By 1800 Flemington was still hardly more than the wide spot of proverb, but as the century progressed the town became a small-scale manufacturing center with iron foundries, glass works, and potteries. Its location also made it a rail nexus for trains running to New York City, Philadelphia, and points west. The first tracks were laid in 1854, and by 1889 more than fifty trains a day ran through town, though not all of them stopped.

It was about this time that some interesting Victorian residences began to arise in the area. Survivors include examples in the Italianate and Stick styles and at least one that defies categorization altogether. The house built for William Edgar Emery should be enough to dispel any misconception that all East Coast houses were models of propriety. It contains a virtual dictionary of late Victorian wooden ornament. The brackets under the eaves are Italianate; the third-story gazebo, Queen Anne; and the gable bracings, Stick style. There are also Moorish arches, a mansardic tower, and incised and applied work that bears the Eastlake stamp. Beneath it all is a meandering wood-frame house as outlandish as anything that ever rose in Texas or California. Now owned by the city, the one-time residence serves as an office building.

EXECUTIVE MANSION
1883-91: Raleigh, North Carolina

During General Sherman's brief stay in Raleigh, his troops so thoroughly ransacked the old Governor's Palace that it was never again used as the home of the chief officer of the state. It was nearly twenty years before legislators got around to building a new executive mansion. When they did, they hired the prominent but elderly Samuel Sloan to design it.

Sloan (1815-84) had begun his long career when he took a job as a journeyman carpenter in Philadelphia in 1836. By the late 1840s he had established himself as an architect, but his star truly began to rise in 1850 when he was engaged to design *Bartram Hall*, the home of a millionaire industrialist. For the next decade he was the favorite architect of the industrial plutocracy that had lately risen in the City of Brotherly Love. During this period his work was consistently featured in *Godey's Lady's Book*. He also published several influential books of house plans, of which *The Model Architect* (1852-53) is the best known today.

It was fortunate for Sloan that these publications helped make his name known beyond the Philadelphia city limits, for a minor scandal in 1860 threw his professional ethics into question and his local practice into a tailspin. After the Civil War he increasingly sought out-of-town commissions and found a healthy market for his talents in the Reconstruction South.

In his work on the Executive Mansion Sloan was assisted by another Philadelphia-based architect, Gustavus Adolphus Bauer, who designed a number of other structures in Raleigh (p. 195) while he waited for work on the mansion to proceed. The plans for the new governor's house had been approved in 1883, but owing to a tight-fisted legislature it was nearly eight years before the building was finished. Sloan died of a stroke before the foundations were laid, and it fell to Bauer to see the project through to completion.

In plan the house displays a penchant for picturesque form that was typical of the late Victorian period. Though symmetrical, the facade is irregular by virtue of its swooping gables and high-flying chimney stacks. There are some touches of the Americanized Eastlake style in the turned posts of the verandas and balconies. But as Mary Mix Foley has suggested, the source of the design may trace to the brick manor houses of the Tudor period with their symmetrical compositions, steep gables, and stone trim.

Materials native to North Carolina were used throughout the mansion. The quoins and belt courses that enliven the red bricks are of locally quarried sandstone, and some of the interior rooms with their lofty, sixteen-foot ceilings are decorated with Carolina marble and heart-of-pine. Much of the construction work was performed by convicts under the direction of W.J. Hicks, superintendent of the state prison, who happened to be an architect and engineer as well. Some of the fine-gauged bricks in the structure still bear the initials of the prisoners who molded them. Today both the Executive Mansion and its gardens are open for tours by the public at varying times throughout the year.

WILDERSTEIN
1852-88: Rhinebeck vicinity, New York

Although the house shown here has maintained the same essential shape and dimensions for the last hundred years, it was once a two-story Italianate villa. A ghost of the original structure that John Warren Ritch designed for Thomas Holy Suckley can still be seen in the wing at left.

When Robert Bowne Suckley inherited the house in the late 1880s, however, he hired a Poughkeepsie architect, Arnout Cannon, Jr., to remodel it. Cannon's work gave rise to the towered, three-story dwelling that stands today. Although he added some new stylistic touches—Eastlake detailing and a lofty Queen Anne tower—some vestiges of the older style are still apparent in the extensive eaves bracketing and the rather formal symmetry of the facade. Currently undergoing restoration, *Wilderstein* stands near the banks of the Hudson as a sort of naked monument to wood-frame construction.

H.W. MERRIAM HOUSE

1884: Newton, New Jersey

This house in the northwestern corner of New Jersey was originally the home of Henry W. Merriam, a shoe manufacturer. He had arrived in Newton in 1870 and set up a small plant that produced its first pair of shoes three years later—just in time for the financial panic that swept the country in 1873. Despite this inauspicious start, his company prospered, and by the end of the century it was the largest manufacturer of footwear in the state, even though it limited its line to "Ladies, misses, and children."

Among the reasons for the firm's success was a small army of salesmen who bypassed wholesalers and dealt directly with shoe stores throughout the country. But Merriam was also, by all accounts, a model employer, keeping the plant running during the financial troubles of the early 1890s and establishing a building-and-loan association which enabled company employees to finance their own homes.

The expansive residence he built for himself in 1884 is a fairly early example of a house type that became enormously popular in the 1890s. Merriam is said to have designed it himself, but it seems more likely that he had some professional help. The house contains almost all the features that came to define the American Queen Anne villa in years to come: irregular plan, horizontal massing, complex hipped roof, a sprinkling of Eastlake applique, and, of course, a corner tower.

These essentials were all part of the original construction of 1883-84, but some other important details were not acquired until the 1890s. According to an early photograph, the porte-cochere and the porches that wrap around the tower on the first and second floors were still missing as of 1891.

After Merriam's death in 1900, the house was acquired by the Presbyterian Church he had attended in town. It is in use today as a home for senior citizens and is open for tours by appointment.

C.M. TRIPP HOUSE
1887: New Bedford, Massachusetts

In New England the Queen Anne style was often more reserved than in other parts of the country. The house shown here has taken on some of the characteristic features of the style but has combined them tastefully and conservatively—as if it were being careful not to offend the neighbors with too gaudy a display.

Some suggestion of the variegated surfaces that were a hallmark of the Queen Anne can be seen in this house. The first floor is sheathed in clapboard, the second story is shingled, and the upper gable contains a herringbone motif reminiscent of the Stick style. In addition, the bow window anticipates the Shingle style. As evidenced by the off-center gable and engaged corner turret, some attempt at picturesque massing has been made. But the central placement of the entryway and its projecting vestibule confirms the essential formality of the structure.

The house was built for Charles M. Tripp, who ran a dry goods store in New Bedford. In 1887 he purchased the lot from William Rotch (p. 18), whose family owned a good deal of real estate in New Bedford. After Tripp's death in 1898, his wife sold the house to Walter H. Langshaw, who managed one of the local cotton mills. Today, after more than a century of use, the house still serves as a private residence.

L.J. FITZGERALD HOUSE

1885: Cortland, New York

The Fitzgerald House is another example of the corner-towered Queen Anne villa, a style and a type already seen in prototypical form in the Merriam House in Newton, New Jersey (p. 185). Though this example was built just a few years later, it displays some interesting new details. The scroll-cut ornament and Eastlake applique of the older house have here given way to spindlework and patterned shingles; and the top-heavy octagonal tower has become rounded, stouter, and more robust looking. The front gable has also become broader and is boxed at the bottom instead of opening into the wall below.

These changes indicate an evolution away from the somewhat spindly Gothic of past decades toward the more full-bodied Queen Anne style of the 1890s.

The house was designed by J.H. Kirby, a Syracuse architect who published at least three house plan books in the 1870s and '80s. It originally belonged to L.C. Fitzgerald, president of the Cortland Wagon Company, the largest of several similar firms in the city. His former residence is currently being converted for use as a sorority house.

ASENDORF HOUSE
1899: Savannah, Georgia

This wood-turner's fantasy come true was originally the home of Cord Asendorf, a German emigrant who left his native Osterholz at the age of fourteen to seek his fortune in America. Arriving in Savannah in 1872, he went to work for an uncle, a grocer who catered to the small German community in town. In time he acquired the wherewithal to marry, open his own store, and to begin dabbling in real estate—proof positive that he had become thoroughly Americanized. He was successful enough at the last occupation to retire at age forty.

The site he chose for his own residence was just outside the city limits at the turn of the century but is now considered almost downtown. To an ordinary gable-roofed builder's box, Asendorf added three extraordinary porches adorned with lathe-turned fancywork—posts, balusters, and spindles—all arranged around a series of basket arches turned sideways. At the front of the house both levels of the double-decker porch are identical, and the side balcony is a compressed version of the same patterning. Asendorf is supposed to have designed these details himself, but the actual work is credited to the Hawley Construction Company.

Turned gingerbread of this sort was popular in many parts of the country until the end of the century and was particularly associated with the Queen Anne style, though it is also, rather misleadingly, called Eastlake.

Originally painted white, the house is now a restrained but attractive yellow, accented with carefully selected pinks and greens to bring out details in the bracketing on the porch and beneath the eaves. Known locally as *The Gingerbread House*, it has been stopping cars for nearly a century, including, as the story goes, Franklin Delano Roosevelt's, back in the 1930s. Though still a private residence, it is open for group tours and receptions by appointment.

GILSON RESIDENCE
1885: Saratoga Springs, New York

Today in use as a funeral parlor, this Queen Anne house in brick was originally the residence of Colonel Joseph Gilson, a lumber dealer from Georgia who spent his summers in Saratoga Springs. It was designed by R. Newton Brezee, who was responsible for several other residences in town. Brezee had begun his career in Saratoga as a carpenter, but in 1884 he hung out a shingle and listed himself in the city directory as an architect.

His design for Gilson is a compact, suburban version of more expansive Queen Anne villas like the Merriam residence (p. 185). Houses of this sort were typically of wood-frame construction: brick was less amenable to the free-flowing plans, variegated surfaces, and curvilinear shapes characteristic of the style. Here the hard-edge geometries of the lower floors are overcome and softened to some extent by wooden details—verandas, balconies, and a tower that sprouts from the top of the canted bay at the corner of the house.

193

CAPEHART HOUSE
1898: Raleigh, North Carolina

Rendered in brick, the corner-towered Queen Anne house has a more castle-like appearance than its counterparts in wood. This example in Raleigh was originally the home of Catherine Moore Capehart, daughter of a prominent North Carolina lawyer, B.F. Moore. Though he had once served as state attorney general, Moore, a strong Unionist, was barred from practicing law in the South when he refused to swear an oath of allegiance to the Confederacy at the outbreak of the Civil War.

Having inherited small fortunes from both her father and her first husband, Kate Moore was a woman of means by the time she married Bartholomew Ashburn "Baldy" Capehart, a well-to-do planter. Precociously for the nineteenth century, the couple signed a prenuptial agreement that stipulated that Mrs. C. would continue to control her own income and property after the marriage. When her new husband died only a few years after the wedding, she found herself thrice rich: in the meantime they had built this fancy new residence in Raleigh.

It was constructed by a contractor named Charles P. Snuggs, who is credited with erecting more than one hundred other structures in the state capital. The design is by Gustavus Adolphus Bauer, who assisted Samuel Sloan in planning the North Carolina Governor's mansion (p. 181).

Considering its brick construction, the house is surprisingly organic and free-flowing in the arrangement of its parts. And it displays a typically Queen Anne taste for variegated surface textures and colors—pressed brick, rough-cut stone, patterned slate, wooden shingles, and stained-glass windows. In addition, the round tower is constructed with curved bricks, and the faces of the octagonal bay are fitted together with knuckle joints.

Moved recently to save it from destruction, the house is now listed on the National Register and is in use as a state office building.

HUNTER HOUSE

c. 1886: Madison, Georgia

Madison, in Morgan County, Georgia, has been a cotton center since its inception. Founded in 1809, it was propitiously located on the stage route from Charleston to New Orleans. Less happily, it was also on the new trail that Sherman's army blazed as it advanced from Atlanta to Savannah in the fall of 1864.

Most of Madison's surviving antebellum homes owe their existence to a resident names Joshua Hill. A United States senator, Hill had resigned his seat rather than vote for secession—as most of his constituents wished him to do. This stand doubtless caused him some difficulties during the war, but it also gave him a bargaining chip when William Tecumseh Sherman showed up on the outskirts of town. The General ended up burning the railroad depot and some small factories but spared most of the houses. As a result, Madison has a wealth of antebellum homes and a tradition of careful preservation that has served to maintain its late-nineteenth-century architecture as well.

The most elaborate residence in town is the Hunter House. It originally belonged to John Hudson Hunter, who built it for his bride shortly after their wedding in 1886. The complex roof forms, rambling plan, and some of the detailing mark it as an example of the Queen Anne style. The small brackets at the cornice, however, are Italianate survivals. The elaborate spindlework and complex, Moorish arches that decorate the porch are thought to be the work of the Atkinson Variety Works, a specialty shop in Madison.

The house has served the Hunter family as a private residence ever since it was built, and the current Mrs. Hunter maintains that it has always been painted white.

W.G. MEANS HOUSE

c. 1890: Concord, North Carolina

According to legend, the seat of Cabarrus County, North Carolina got its name when squabbling settlers, mostly German and Scots-Irish, patched up their differences and named the new community Concord. Hence, also, Union Street, the main thoroughfare in town.

Today the Union Street Historical Districts boast several dozen residences from the late Victorian era. One of them, the Means House, is interesting as yet another variation on the corner-tower theme. In this example the lower walls of the tower have evaporated away, leaving just a bullet-shaped roof to shelter a small second-story balcony. The geometric patterning that decorates the tower frieze and the large projecting bay are also unusual and noteworthy. Still a private residence, the house originally belonged to William G. Means (1850-1918), a Concord attorney who served two terms as mayor and one as state senator in the late 1880s and early '90s.

Too young to have fought in the Civil War, Means is nonetheless remembered as "Colonel." Perhaps he participated in some other conflict, but not necessarily. As an eighteenth-century English tourist noted: "Wherever you travel in Maryland (as also in Virginia and Carolina) your ears are constantly astonished at the number of colonels, majors, and captains that you hear mentioned: in short the whole country seems at first to you a retreat of heroes."

VICTORIA

c. 1890s: Charlotte, North Carolina

Charlotte, the largest urban center in the Carolinas, has paid for its twentieth-century success with the loss of much of its nineteenth-century architecture. The house shown here is one of the few survivors from Tryon Street, which in the 1880s and '90s was the center of the city's most fashionable residential district. In the early-twentieth century, however, most of the fine old houses on the street were destroyed to make way for progress. This one managed to survive only because it was moved to a new location.

The house was originally one of a pair of identical residences built by a local businessman, R.M. Miller, for his two sons—R.M., Jr. and John W. The former's house was eventually destroyed to accommodate urban development, but John's was saved when it was mule-hauled several miles to its present location.

Though no information on who designed the two houses has surfaced thus far, it is apparent that they were planned to complement one another. The missing mate may help explain the unusual treatment of the survivor. Imagining the house in tandem with a twin helps flesh out the curiously undeveloped composition in which the corner tower is half swallowed by the front gable.

As befits one of the last survivors of Charlotte's nineteenth-century past, *Victoria* is in fine condition on the outside. And the interiors contain period furnishings and fittings as well as original Eastlake woodwork and American encaustic tiles. Now listed on the National Register of Historic Places, it is open for group tours by appointment.

T.G. HENDERSON HOUSE
c. 1891: Lake City, Florida

Among the most prolific and successful residential architects of the nineteenth century was George Franklin Barber (1854-1915). Largely self taught, he never attended architecture school, but he did acquire a practical background in ornamental gardening and house carpentry before hanging out his shingle in the late 1880s. His first design projects include some houses that were erected in De Kalb, Illinois by his older brother, a contractor; but it was his mail-order business that brought him ultimate success.

This had its beginnings in 1887 when some of his designs appeared in the trade journal *Carpentry and Building*. Soon afterwards he began receiving orders for working drawings. It was in Knoxville, Tennessee, where he settled around 1890, however, that his operations began in earnest. In 1900, at the peak of his career, he had to employ thirty draftsmen and twenty secretaries to deal with the mail orders and inquiries that arrived at his office each day.

Like George Palliser, the first American architect to base his business primarily on the mails, Barber relied heavily on books and periodicals to attract customers. From the late 1880s until about 1908 he published a series of portfolios and catalogues as well as his own magazine, *American Homes*, in an effort to reach potential clients. All of these publications featured Barber's ever-increasing assortment of designs for "artistic cottage residences" in the latest styles. Readers who liked a particular plan were invited to order detailed working drawings and specifications to be used in construction. Once these left his office, Barber's role in the building process was over, but he felt that his instructions were so clear and complete that they could be followed by any good builder.

The soundness of this approach to architectural marketing is evidenced by the thousands of Barber Houses that were erected in the United States and elsewhere in the final decades of the nineteenth century. Exactly how many have survived to the present is anyone's guess, though one researcher claims to have identified 175 of them. Even if this number were halved, it would be hard to name another nineteenth-century architect who could claim a similar record.

The house shown here was based on "Design No. 56" in Barber's *Cottage Souvenir No. 2* (1890-91). It was built by T.G. Henderson, a wealthy grocer and developer who was known as the "Rockefeller" of Lake City, a small town in north central Florida. In the early 1890s, presumably after seeing the design in print, Henderson ordered plans and specifications from Barber's Knoxville offices, and, serving as his own general contractor, built the house himself. In its essentials it follows the published plan closely, but there are some differences. Some of the ornamental details have been altered and simplified, and the raised foundation shown in the drawing has been eliminated.

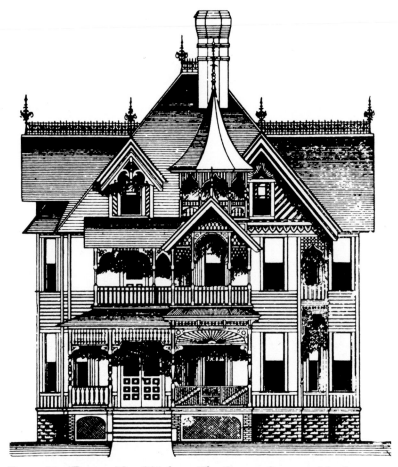

Figure 11: "Design No. 56," from *The Cottage Souvenir No. 2*.

"I cannot speak too strongly in regard to the attractiveness of this design," wrote the architect. "The veranda, balconies and open tower top present a magnificent appearance and afford such an opportunity for extensive views that the house is admirably adapted for a sea-side, lake-shore, or river-view location."

At thirty-eight dollars, "No. 56" was one of the more expensive plans in Barber's book, but it seems to have been quite popular nonetheless. Besides this Florida example, houses based on the same design can still be seen in California, Illinois, Oregon, and Tennessee.

W.B. TITMAN HOUSE
1891: Belvidere, New Jersey

George Franklin Barber's designs were perhaps most popular in the South and Midwest, but scattered examples can also be found on the East Coast. This house, which seems to be based on "Design No. 53" in his *Cottage Souvenir No. 2* (1890-91), was built for William Blair Titman, a banker and the president of the West Jersey Toll Line Company.

The former Titman house, still a private residence, is one of a number of nineteenth-century structures in Belvidere, an attractive small town on the Delaware River. Construction was by Reeder S. Emery, a local builder who presumably worked from plans ordered from Barber's firm in Knoxville. Of special note is the circular front window with rectangular insert and matching spider's-web spindlework on the porch. The house is a mirror reversal of the published design, and it seems also to be somewhat abbreviated in width. Such deviations from plan were not unusual in Barber Houses: the architect stressed that all his designs could be "enlarged, reduced or changed to front in any direction."

Figure 12: "Design No. 53," from *The Cottage Souvenir No. 2.*

QUEEN ANNE HOUSE
c. 1895: Lancaster, New Hampshire

To follow up on the success of his *Cottage Souvenir* series, George Franklin Barber began publishing a monthly magazine in January 1895. *American Homes* remained in his hands until 1902, when it moved to New York City. In the meantime it served as a vehicle for generating mail-order business for his firm in Knoxville. Although the magazine went to considerable lengths to provide genuine editorial content for its readers, Barber's designs were prominently featured in every issue.

This house in the north of New Hampshire seems to be based on a plan that was featured in the magazine's premiere issue. Notwithstanding some differences—in the roof particularly—it bears a strong resemblance to the published drawing. Some of the porch details, indeed, are too similar to be the result of mere happenstance. M.A. Tomlan, who has made an extensive study of Barber Houses, has uncovered examples similar to this one in Alabama and upstate New York, so the design may have been a fairly popular one.

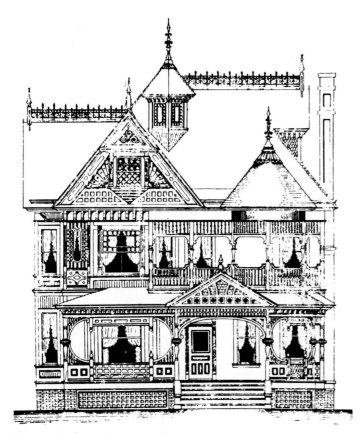

Figure 13: from *American Homes*.

PENN HOUSE

c. 1896: Danville, Virginia

"It's a mighty rough road from Lynchburg to Danville, and she's lying on a three mile grade." Besides Old 97 which crashed there in 1903, Danville's major claim to fame is that it was the last capital of the Confederacy—Jefferson Davis and his staff set up headquarters in town after the fall of Richmond in April 1865. But it is also known as a tobacco and textile center. The Dan River that flows nearby gave its name to both the town and its most important mill.

In the late nineteenth and early twentieth centuries scores of minor mansions, the residences of mill owners and tobacco men, sprang up on Main Street, a section of which came to be known as Millionaires' Row, now a designated historical district. Many of these houses were of brick construction and were decorated with frilly iron work, but this example, the home of a local lumber dealer, was naturally constructed of wood. The spindle course on the porch contains more than 250 lathe-turned pieces and there are an equal number of balusters supporting the railing.

An examplar of the corner-towered Queen Anne, the house was built for Peter C. Penn (1848-1911), a tobacco planter who got into the lumber business after moving to Danville in the 1890s. The design as well as the construction has been attributed to James Huey Fitzgerald, who seems to have been a local builder. Nearly razed in the 1970s to make room for yet another parking lot, the house was restored by new owners and is still in use as a private residence.

DAVIS-JOHNSEY HOUSE

c. 1898: Laurens, South Carolina

Resolutely traditional in its architecture, South Carolina did not, in general, embrace Victoriana with open arms. Charleston, in particular, clung to the old forms even while rebuilding after the Civil War. Upcountry in the Piedmont, however, this traditional bias seems to have held less sway, to judge from the numerous late Victorian houses that can still be found in smaller towns.

This example in Laurens was designed by an architect who is remembered only by the name Owens. It is, nonetheless, a fine example of the corner-towered Queen Anne, and displays most of the requisites that define the style: hipped roof, wraparound porch and attached gazebo, turned balusters, extensive spindle courses, even a touch of Eastlake applique. It was built for David Ashmore Davis (1860-1916) who owned a dry goods store in town. And in 1937, it became the home of Andrew H. Johnsey, a cotton merchant and broker with whose family it has remained ever since.

Laurens, a cotton and textile center, was founded in 1785, but the area had been settled about thirty years before that. The first white pioneer is thought to have been one John Duncan, who came down the Blueridge from Pennsylvania around 1755. Both the town and the surrounding county are named for Henry Lauren of Charleston—a "sterling patriot," "distinguished warrior," and "sagacious statesman"—who served as President of the Continental Congress during the Revolutionary War.

NEW HAYWOOD

c. 1890: Washington, Georgia

Immediately after Lee's surrender at Appomattox, *Haywood*, the home of the staunchly southern Andrews family, became a temporary haven for principals of the Confederacy who felt the need to disappear for a while. The house itself disappeared somewhere down the line but was replaced, symbolically at least, by *New Haywood*, which was built for Theoderic M. Green in the early 1890s.

The design, which has been attributed to the Atlanta architect E.T. Lind, displays most of the features associated with the late Queen Anne style. Besides the irregularity of silhouette and plan, not to mention some nice lathework on the porch, the house is notable for its octagonal bay with third-story gazebo—a regional adaptation of the more common corner tower. Still a private residence, *New Haywood* is located in Washington's Robert Toombs Historic District, where a number of other residences, Victorian and antebellum, can also be found.

QUEEN ANNE HOUSE

c. 1895: Rutland, Vermont

This house seems to have been built for Frank Houghton, a dry good merchant in Rutland, and it once belonged to the Meldon Sisters, who are remembered as "a couple of old maids," but nothing is known of who designed it.

Not that it really matters at this point, of course. Houses like this one had become so common in America by the mid-1890s that any builder worth his saltbox could have put one together from the stock plans, pattern books, and prefabricated details in his bag of tricks. Versions of the same hipped-roof, corner-towered house seen here can be found from Maryland to California. Far from the leading edge of architectural taste, the Queen Anne style had become as homely and comfortable as a Rockwell painting.

In the twenty years since the style had arrived in the United States, architects like Henry Hobson Richardson, McKim, Mead, and White, and others had abandoned it for high-style experiments in the Shingle and Romanesque styles. But during the same period the low-art crowd—carpenters, and architects who had graduated from their ranks—were modifying the boxy English prototypes to create a house type that appealed enormously to American taste. The result was a new sort of Queen Anne, broad-beamed and rambling, with towers, balconies, wraparound porches and a lot of fussy details. Beneath this "flummery," as John Maas called it, was an eminently livable house, soundly constructed, convenient, and "planned from the inside out."

QUEEN ANNE HOUSE
1894: Pittsford, New York

This house in Pittsford, a small town near Rochester, is perhaps typical of the modest Queen Anne residences that can still be seen in communities from New York to California. For many Americans in the late nineteenth century such houses represented the domestic ideal, the rose-covered cottage of popular song.

Houses like this one maintained only tenuous connections with the Queen Anne originals that had arrived from England in the mid-1870s. Here, there are only hints of the horizontal massing and busy surface details that characterized early versions of the style. The corner tower has shrunk to an open pavilion at one side of the veranda, and the ornamental excess of years past has been reduced to a few chaste details—shingles and vestigial Eastlake motifs in the gables; lathe-turned posts, balusters, and spindles on the porch. Still, it retains the organic arrangement of parts that made such houses so eminently livable.

The house was constructed, probably from stock plans, by a pair of local builders named William Hetzer and George Hooker. It was originally owned by one Granden Vought, and for many years it was the home of a local doctor. After nearly a hundred years of life, it is still serving as a private residence.

C.F. WICKWIRE HOUSE

1890: Cortland, New York

This thirty-room mansion was built as the home of Chester Franklin Wickwire, a wealthy manufacturer from upstate New York. It is, nonetheless, essentially a New York City house. While visiting Manhattan in 1888, Wickwire was struck by a residence that had recently been completed for James Anthony Bailey—P.T. Barnum's partner—and contacted the architect who had designed it. Samuel Burrage Reed, who published a number of pattern books in the 1880s and '90s, prepared plans for Wickwire that virtually mirrored the Bailey house.

Aptly named, Wickwire (1843-1910) had made his fortune from the manufacture of woven wire products and metal cloth. Born near Cortland, he began his career as a grocer but soon switched to the retail hardware business. Tinkering with an old carpet loom that he had taken as payment for a bad debt, he invented a wire-weaving machine and obtained a patent that was basic to the process of weaving metals. He might have become moderately wealthy simply by selling these rights, but he chose instead to establish his own plant in which he began manufacturing such products as window screens and wire fences. By the time he built his stone mansion, he had expanded this facility into a large factory complex complete with its own open-hearth steel plant and wire-drawing facilities.

The house was constructed of Indiana limestone and is said to have cost $75,000 to build. A typically eclectic product of the late nineteenth century, it contains hints of a half dozen styles, with Romanesque features predominating. Hallmarks of the style include the rough stone construction, round-headed tower windows, and Roman arches that form an arcaded loggia. Other notable features include the carved stone belt course, the castellated bay to the rear of the house, and the amazing little bartizan which clings to one corner of the facade. The shaped gables are reminiscent of forms that can be seen in Chateauesque, Dutch, and even California Mission Revival houses.

The mansion remained in the possession of Wickwire's heirs until the early 1970s when it was acquired by the Landmark Society of Cortland County. In 1975 it was opened to the public as *The 1890 House Museum and Center for Victorian Arts*. The interiors contain fine woodwork, elaborate wall stenciling, period furnishings, and rare glass chandeliers from the firm of J.B. Tiffany, nephew of Louis Comfort. The Bailey House, incidentally, has been designated a New York City Landmark and is said to be the last freestanding Victorian mansion in Manhattan.

CHRISTIAN HEURICH HOUSE
1892-94: Washington, D.C.

Now the headquarters of the Columbia Historical Society, this Romanesque castle was originally the home of Christian Heurich (1842-1944), a brewer who became one of the wealthiest citizens in the nation's capital. It was designed by the Washington architect John Granville Meyers, who—in this case, at least—was strongly influenced by the work of Henry Hobson Richardson.

Richardson was the second American architect to graduate from the Ecole des Beaux-Arts in Paris, and he pioneered the use of the Romanesque style in the United States. When added to the mulligan stew of late-nineteenth-century design, his fusion of Gothic and Roman forms gave rise to a new stylistic dish, the Richardsonian Romanesque, which was employed most frequently in large government buildings but was also popular as a house style for the very wealthy.

The Heurich House illustrates some of the defining features of the style: massive construction in brick and rough-cut stone; polychromatic interplays of red brick, brownstone, and verdigris; broad Roman arches; deeply recessed windows; and, of course, the obligatory tower.

The formidable, castle-like effect of this and similar houses of the Gilded Age suggests that psychologically, at least, some of the very rich were getting ready for a siege. Heurich, however, had some slender excuse for building so monumentally in that he had been born in a similar structure in Germany. For a few years he and his innkeeper parents occupied part of a genuine castle that dated from before The Thirty Years' War.

Orphaned while still in his teens, Heurich took to the road and supported himself by working in breweries in a half dozen European capitals. By the time he arrived in Washington in 1866 he had all the expertise he needed to start his own business. Serving as his own brewmaster, kettleman, engineer, agent, and collector, he worked eighteen hours a day and within a few years found himself the owner of the most successful brewery in the city.

Part of his success owed to the fact that he had perfected a lager that was more in accord with American taste than the darker English beers that had dominated the market up to the 1840s. But Heurich himself attributed much of his good fortune to advertising.

In those days advertisements were not required to adhere even marginally to the truth. One of his ads, for instance, claimed that Heurich's Beer was "Recommended for family use by physicians generally." He also contrived to have testimonials for the beverage inserted into straight news stories. Thus a *Washington Post* article on a local divorce segued blithely into the assertion that "Nothing else promotes domestic peace and happiness like Heurich's Beer."

As he became wealthier, Heurich invested heavily in real estate but mistrusted the stock market. He often visited Europe and is said to have crossed the Atlantic no less than seventy-three times. At Bayreuth he saw *Parsifal* and met Wagner, and he also exchanged letters with Hindenburg. During the First World War his recent visits to the fatherland caused him some trouble. Rumors circulated that he was in wireless communication with the Kaiser and that his Maryland farm harbored artillery pieces which were trained on the Capitol. He countered these stories by starting a rumor of his own that he had committed suicide.

Actually, he lived to be 102 and claimed in his later years that his own beer was the source of his longevity.

In 1956, Heurich's family donated the mansion to the Columbia Historical Society for use as a museum and library. It still contains much of its original furniture and trappings and is open for tours by the public.

221

CHATEAUESQUE HOUSE

1896-98: New Haven, Connecticut

This house was originally built for Merritt W. Burwell, a businessman who was listed in the New Haven city directory of 1895 as a contractor, real-estate speculator, and the president of the Marine Engineering Company. Flushed with success in the mid-1890s, Burwell commissioned the Bridgeport architect Joseph W. Northrop to design a residence befitting his economic status and the social station he apparently coveted. His new residence was planned for New Haven's fashionable Whitney Avenue, and no expense, as they say, was spared. The result was a three-story demi-mansion of brick with copper trim on the facade and spacious interiors that included a third-story ballroom.

Northrop's earlier work had included some rather fine residences in the Queen Anne and Shingle modes, but the house he designed for Burwell must be accounted his masterpiece. It is an example of the late French Gothic or Chateauesque style that epitomized affluent taste in America at the close of the century. It was the same style that Richard Morris Hunt had incorporated in the design of a number of millionaires' mansions. Burwell's house, in fact, resembled Hunt's William K. Vanderbilt House on Fifth Avenue in two particulars that virtually define the Chateauesque—a tall hipped roof and a prominent dormer with a characteristic shield-like surround.

In some other respects the Burwell house is less beholden to French models. The inviting, commodious porch that wraps around the front and side of the house, for example, is characteristically American. But despite this homey touch, the overall effect of the structure is awe-inspiring, fortress-like, defensive. The brick construction, heavy oak doors, and engaged towers on both sides of the facade suggest that Burwell may have been expecting a siege.

Which, in fact, may have been the case. Construction costs had strained his resources beyond their limits, and he had to borrow at least twenty-thousand dollars to complete the house. Meanwhile, his various business enterprises had turned sour. In the end he occupied his new residence scarcely twelve months before liens and foreclosure bade him depart. In 1900, according to the directory, he was living in a rooming house and working as a traveling salesman. Two years later he was not listed at all.

In the ninety years since Burwell's demise the house has changed hands several times. A civil engineer named Colin Ingersoll bought it from a speculator in the early 1900s; and for much of the twentieth century it was the home of a family that the cartoonist Charles Adams might have had fun with—the well-to-do Linahans, proprietors of the National Casket Company. More recently, in 1971, the former Burwell house was acquired by the Pellegrini Law Firm of New Haven. It has since been refurbished and converted for use as offices. The expansive but seldom used ballroom now serves as a private law library.

223

BURRAGE MANSION
1899: Boston, Massachusetts

Once a swampy marshland, Boston's Back Bay was "reclaimed" from nature to be developed as a residential area. This was largely due to the efforts of Arthur Gilman (1821-82), an influential architect and planner who was himself strongly influenced by Andrew Jackson Downing. His fondness for the Italian Renaissance and French Second Empire styles is reflected in many of the houses that were built in the area after the Civil War.

Commonwealth Avenue, the most stylish street in the Back Bay, contains some of the most elegant and best preserved nineteenth-century town and rowhouses in the country. The lines of fine houses on each block are bracketed by especially sumptuous mansions at the corners of the intersecting streets. The one shown here was originally the home of Boston millionaire Albert Burrage and was designed by Charles E. Brigham (1841-1925) who had worked for Gilman earlier in his career. By the 1890s he was an established architect in Boston. Today he is remembered primarily for some of the large public buildings he designed.

The Burrage mansion was a bit out of the ordinary for restrained Boston, which generally preferred simpler forms to the sort of New York finery seen here. Constructed of limestone, the house is modeled after *Chenonceaux*, a chateau in the Loire Valley. Besides the characteristically steep roof and ornate dormer windows, it has a pair of engaged towers and a range of carved ornamental details from the French Gothic—gnomes, dragons, chimera, cherubs, and so forth. The interiors are even more sumptuous and still contain an ornately sculpted marble staircase, stained-glass windows, and gold-leafed ceiling decoration. The mansion is now in use as the Boston Evening Clinic, a progressive institution that dates to the 1920s when it was established by Doctor Morris Cohen to meet the health-care needs of day workers.

225

THE BREAKERS

1895: Newport, Rhode Island

One of the grandest of the vacation palaces erected in Newport during the Gilded Age was *The Breakers*, the summer home of Cornelius Vanderbilt II, one of the Commodore's grandsons. It was designed, of course, by Richard Morris Hunt, who made his reputation building mansions, mausoleums, and summer homes for the Vanderbilts, the Astors, the Goelets and a few other members of the New York-Newport Four Hundred.

Hunt (1827-1895) was born the son of a congressman in Brattlesboro, Vermont and spent his early years in New Haven and Boston. In 1846 he became the first American to be admitted to the Ecole des Beaux-Arts in Paris. In all he spent six years in Europe, supplementing his formal studies with travels in Italy, the Middle East, and the Loire Valley. During this period he acquired architectural ideas and inspiration that would last him the rest of his career.

After establishing a practice in New York in 1857, Hunt helped pioneer the Stick style with his design for the Griswold House in Newport (1863), but he had to wait a few years before he could exercise his true proclivities for grandeur with a French accent. His first major opportunity came when he was commissioned to design a town house for William Kissam Vanderbilt in 1879. The building that arose to greet an astonished Fifth Avenue was the incarnation of a sixteenth-century French chateau in grey Indiana limestone.

Its unparalleled opulence may or may not have helped the upstart Vanderbilts attain the inner circle of New York society, but it definitely placed Hunt at the pinnacle of American architecture. For the rest of his days he was a favorite of millionaires and a particular favorite of the Commodore's numerous offspring.

Though his preferred style was the refined and rarified Gothic of the Chateauesque, Hunt's design for *The Breakers* recalls the Renaissance *palazzi* of northern Italy. Both the overall plan and the details are formal, classically correct, and carefully balanced. Along with the piers and columns and formal loggias are carved garlands, swags, and festoons. And the incredibly sumptuous interiors—all marbles and onyx, bronze, crystal, and gilt—are a story in themselves.

Today *The Breakers* is open for public tours under the auspices of the Preservation Society of Newport County and is well worth seeing if only because it was one of the houses that helped usher in a new era of classicism in American architecture. By the end of the century the Victorian romanticism that had held sway for more than fifty years had nearly spent itself, and the way was open for further developments. While a new architecture was brewing in the Chicago of Louis Sullivan and Frank Lloyd Wright, the architectural establishment was once again taking refuge in the classical past.

227

BILTMORE
1895: Asheville, North Carolina

In the 1850s A.J. Downing had confidently asserted that great American fortunes would be dispersed within a generation or so of their making. This idea was plausible enough as far as it went, but it failed to reckon with the enormous accumulation of wealth that was to occur during the Gilded Age. In the 1850s a man who had a million dollars was a rarity; by the end of the century, real wealth was counted in multimillions.

When he died Commodore Vanderbilt possessed not merely one but a *hundred* million dollars. And far from squandering the family fortune, his son William Henry more than doubled it in something less than a decade. When a mere eighteenth of the accumulated wealth trickled down to George Washington Vanderbilt, one of the Commodore's grandsons, he was able to build one of the largest and most elaborate mansions ever erected in the United States, even if he did have to dip into principal to do it.

Called *Biltmore*, the estate consisted of an enormous French chateau set in exemplary surroundings—130,000 acres of hills and dales in the Great Smoky Mountains of western North Carolina. In lesser hands the whole thing might have been a disaster. Fortunately G.W.V. was able to command some of the best architectural talent in the country.

Creating this enormous estate cost between four and five million nineteenth-century dollars, and the mansion alone took a thousand workers five years to build. During construction the estate had its own mill and brick foundry not to mention a private railroad spur which linked it with nearby Asheville. Meanwhile, Vanderbilt scoured Europe for art treasures and returned with paintings and artifacts bearing such names as Durer, Meissen, Pelligrini, Sargent.

The mansion itself was designed by Richard Morris Hunt, who took inspiration from the great chateaux of the Loire Valley. Though not strictly symmetrical, the facade is formally balanced with a central entry tower dominating the composition. The steep hipped roofs and parapeted dormers are, of course, hallmarks of the Chateauesque.

When completed, the huge house covered five acres of ground and contained an indoor swimming pool, a bowling alley, and 250 rooms. Its upkeep required no less than eighty servants. *Biltmore* was formally opened on Christmas Eve, 1895, but Richard Morris Hunt was not in attendance. He had died a few months before.

The elaborate landscaping was the work of the formidably talented Frederick Law Olmsted (1822-1903), who had helped lay out Central Park, among other wonders. At *Biltmore* he balanced the formal gardens and terraces around the house with more casual plantings further afield. And he also laid out a long winding road which, in the best tradition of the picturesque, permitted surprise views of the castle at selected bends and curves.

Olmsted, an early conservationist, had been one of the first Americans to urge the creation of a wilderness reserve in the Yosemite Valley, and he also recommended that *Biltmore* be maintained as a natural arboretum. Vanderbilt assented and inaugurated the practice of scientific forest management in America when he engaged a newly trained forester to look after his woodlands. This was Gifford Pinchot who later became Director of the Bureau of Forestry under Teddy Roosevelt.

Though Biltmore has been pared down considerably since the turn of the century, it still encompasses many acres of formal and informal gardens. And the house itself contains some of the most extraordinary and sumptuous interiors in the country. Both the mansion and grounds are now available for public tours.

About the Author

Kenneth Naversen is a freelance writer and photographer whose work has appeared in many national publications. He is a former recipient of an Arts Critic Fellowship from the National Endowment for the Arts and holds a masters degree in Art and Photography. For the past dozen years he has been working as an architectural and advertising photographer from bases in Southern California and the Northwest. His previous book, *West Coast Victorians*, was published by Beautiful America© in 1987.

Acknowledgements

The author and publisher would like to thank the numerous people who helped make this book possible. We are particularly grateful to the many Victorian owners who generously shared information about their houses. The following individuals and groups were especially vital sources of help and information:

Richard L. Ament, Jr., Bethlehem, Pennsylvania — Bob & Gerri Atherton, Richford, Vermont — Peter Bickford, Historic District Association, Richfield Springs, New York — Catherine Bishir, Raleigh, North Carolina — The Brick Store Museum, Kennebunk, Maine — Mrs. Florence Brigham, Historical Society, Fall River, Massachusetts — John K. Bullard, New Bedford, Massachusetts — Mary Burnett, Potomac, Maryland — Mrs. Neil Chambers, Ocean Grove, New Jersey — Leslie Chatterton, Landmarks Preservation Commission, Ithaca, New York — Columbia Historical Society, Washington, D.C. — John Conlin, Landmark Society of the Niagara Frontier, Buffalo — K. Conlin, Windsor Historical Society, Windsor, Vermont — Marianne J. Curling, Curator, Mark Twain Memorial, Hartford — Sherman Currie, Belvidere, New Jersey — Delaware Bureau of Archaeology & Historic Preservation — Mrs. Daniel Denny, Savannah, Georgia — Richard J. Devine, Newton, New Jersey — Sally Dickerson, Gainesville, Florida — Joan M. Doerr, Buffalo, New York — Mark Dolhopf & Marjo Anderson, New Haven, Connecticut — The Essex Institute, Salem, Massachusetts — The Executive Mansion, Raleigh, North Carolina — Fairfield Historical Society, Fairfield, Connecticut — Florida State Division of Historical Resources — Herb & Jan Galloway, Savannah — James L. Garvin, New Hampshire Division of Historical Resources — Francis M. Gay, Charlotte, North Carolina — Georgia Historical Society, Savannah — Mrs. Andrew God, Lake City, Florida — Sheilagh Nolan Guyer, Thomaston, Maine — Mark W. Haag, Ithaca, New York — Patricia Handwerk, Jim Thorpe, Pennsylvania — John Herzan, Connecticut Historical Commission — Sara & Herman Hirsh, Cape May, New Jersey — Byron B. Holmes, Historical Society of Ocean Grove, New Jersey — Cynthia Howk, Landmark Society of Western New York, Rochester — Mrs. Nathan Hudson Hunter, Madison, Georgia — Hunterdon County Cultural & Heritage Commission, Flemington, New Jersey — Joseph E. Illick Jr., Coopersburg, Pennsylvania — Alfreda Irwin, The Chautauqua Institution, Chautauqua, New York — Mrs. Mary

F. Johnsey, Laurens, South Carolina — Caroline Kellem, Commission for Historical & Architectural Preservation, City of Baltimore — Bill & Helene Kennann, Long Beach, California — Professor James K. Kettlewell, Skidmore College, Saratoga Springs, New York — Dean Kimmel, Peale Museum, Baltimore — Mrs. Gretchen Kingsley, Branford, Connecticut — Joe Krause, California State University, Long Beach — Margaret Ladd, Gothic Cottage Restoration Committee, Cazenovia, New York — Laurens County Library, Laurens, South Carolina — Lockwood-Mathews Mansion Museum, Norwalk, Connecticut — Joseph Pell Lombardi, New York, New York — A. Arthur Lowenthal, Caldwell, New Jersey — Maine Historic Preservation Commission — Massachusetts Historical Commission — Doris Masten, Delamater House, Rhinebeck, New York — Thomas & Harriet McGraw, Windsor, Vermont — Taylor McMillan, Raleigh, North Carolina — J. Robert Mello, Fort Lauderdale, Florida — Col. & Mrs. John Miller, Leesburg, Virginia — Kathy S. Moses, Ebenezer Maxwell Mansion, Philadelphia — National Register of Historic Places, Department of the Interior — Christopher Nevins, Fairfield Historical Society, Connecticut — Robert & Susan Naversen, Greenwich, Connecticut — Ronald Naversen, Carbondale, Illinois — Rare Books & Manuscripts Division, New York Public Library — John Nozynski, The 1890 House Museum, Cortland, New York — Austin O'Brien, New York State Office of Historic Preservation — Jeff O'Dell, Department of Historic Resources, Commonwealth of Virginia — Ray & Rainy Peden, New Castle, Delaware — Bernard A. Pellegrino, New Haven, Connecticut — Pennsylvania Bureau for Historic Preservation, Harrisburg — Mr. & Mrs. William A. Pope, Washington, Georgia — Preservation Society of Newport County — Providence Preservation Society — Arnold Robinson, Office of Housing & Neighborhood Development, City of New Bedford, Massachusetts — Roseland Cottage, Woodstock, Connecticut — Robert W. Ryerss Library, Philadelphia — Jay & Marianne Schatz, Cape May, New Jersey — Robert M.

Shinn, Concord, North Carolina — Gunny & Arlene Skarkarl, Long Island, New York — Mrs. Doris Soucy, Newnan, Georgia — Michael T. Southern, North Carolina State Office of Historic Preservation — Phinizy Spalding, Athens, Georgia — Frank Spear, Warner Robbins, Georgia — Sussex County Library, Newton, New Jersey — Charles & Priscilla Thompson, Springfield, Virginia — Richard Tyler, Philadelphia Historical Commission — Glen Uminowicz, Executive Director, Morse-Libby House, Portland, Maine — The University of the South, Sewanee, Tennessee — Vermont Division for Historic Preservation — Victorian Society of America, Philadelphia — T. Michael Ward, Newport Beach, California — Dane & Joan Wells, Cape May, New Jersey — Charles & Pauline Webber, Salem, Virginia — Jean L. Werner, Rutland, Vermont — Lynne Wiley, Pembroke, New Hampshire — The Robert Winnebrenner family, Pittsford, New York — Winslow Library, Winslow, Maine — Mrs. Julian Bradford Woelfel, Columbus, Ohio.

ILLUSTRATION CREDITS

Figure 4 courtesy Historic American Buildings Survey, National Park Service. Figure 6 courtesy The Library of Congress. Figures 10, 11, 12, 13, courtesy The American Life Foundation, Box 349, Watkins Glen, New York 14891.

Bibliography

Allentown Association, Inc. *A Field Guide to the Architecture and History of Allentown*. Buffalo: By the Association, 1987.

Andrews, Wayne. *American Gothic: Its Origins, Its Trials, Its Triumphs*. New York: Random House, 1975.

_____. *Architecture, Ambition and Americans: A Social History of American Architecture* (1947). New York: Glencoe/ MacMillan, 1964.

Ames, Winslow. "The Transformation of Chateau-sur-Mer." *Journal of the Society of Architectural Historians* 24:4 December 1970.

Barber, George Franklin. *The Cottage Souvenir No. 2*. Knoxville: S.B. Newman & Co., 1890-91: Reprint with new introduction by Michael A. Tomlan. Watkins Glen: American Life Foundation, 1982.

Cahill, Mary and Grant, Gary. *Victorian Danville: Fifty-two Landmarks: Their Architecture & History*. Danville, Virginia: Womack Press, 1977.

Clayton, Barbara and Whitley, Kathleen. *A Guide to New Bedford*. Montpelier, VT: Capitol City Press.

Croff, Gilbert Bostwick. *Progressive American Architecture*. New York: Orange Judd, 1875.

Cromie, Alice. *Restored America*. New York: American Legacy Press, 1979.

Davidson, Marshall. *History of Notable American Houses*. New York: American Heritage Publishing Company, 1971.

Davis, Alexander Jackson. *Rural Residences*. New York: By the Author, 1838. Reprint with new introduction by Jane Davies. New York: Da Capo Press, 1980.

Dictionary of American Biography. New York: Scribner, 1928-58.

Dorsey, John and Dilts, James D. *A Guide to Baltimore Architecture*. Centreville, MD: Tidewater Publishers, 1981.

Downing, Andrew Jackson. *The Architecture of Country Houses*. New York: D. Appleton & Co., 1850. Reprint with introduction by J. Stewart Johnson. New York: Dover, 1969.

_____. *Cottage Residences*. New York: John Wiley & Son, 1842, 1873. Reprinted as *Victorian Cottage Residences*, New York: Dover, 1981.

_____. *A Treatise on the Theory and Practice of Landscape Gardening*. 2nd ed. New York: Wiley & Putnam, 1844.

Downing, Antoinette F. and Scully, Vincent. *The Architectural Heritage of Newport, Rhode Island*. Cambridge: Harvard University Press, 1952.

Eberlein, Harold D. and Hubbard, Cortland. *Historic Houses and Buildings of Delaware*. Dover: Public Archives Commission, 1962.

Encyclopedia of Architects. Adolf K. Placzek, Editor: New York: MacMillan, 1982.

Foley, Mary Mix. *The American House*. New York: Harper & Row, 1980.

Fowler, Orson Squire. *A Home for all, or The gravel wall and Octagon Mode of Building. . .* New York: Fowlers & Wells, 1853. Reprint with introduction by Madeleine B. Stern. New York: Dover, 1973.

Furnas, J.C. *The Americans: A Social History of the United States, 1547-1914*. New York: G.P. Putnam's Sons, 1969.

Garvin, James L. *Historic Portsmouth: Early Photographs from the Collections of Strawbery Banke Inc*. Somersworth: New Hampshire Publishing Company, 1974.

Gilpatrick, George A. *Kennebunk History*. Kennebunk, Maine: Star Print, 1939.

Gottfried, Herbert and Jennings, Jan. *American Vernacular Design 1870-1940: An Illustrated Glossary*. New York: Van Nostrand, 1985.

Gowans, Alan. *Architecture in New Jersey: A Record of American Civilization*. Princeton: D. Van Nostrand & Company, 1964.

Henneman, John Bell. "George Rainsford Fairbanks." *The Sewanee Review Quarterly*, October 1906.

Hitchcock, Henry-Russell. *American Architectural Books*. Minneapolis: University of Minnesota, 1946, 1962.

Hobbs, Isaac H. and Son. *Hobbs' Architecture*. Philadelphia: J.B. Lippincott & Co., 1873.

Hourihan, Chip. *Federal Hill: A Series of Walking Tours*. Bristol, Connecticut: City of Bristol, 1985.

Jacobsen, Hugh Newell (ed.) *A Guide to the Architecture of Washington, D.C.* New York: Praeger, 1963.

James, Henry. *The Art of Travel*. New York: Doubleday, 1958.

Lane, Mills. *Architecture of the Old South: Virginia*. Savannah: The Beehive Press, 1987.

Linley, John. *The Georgia Catalog: Historic American Building Survey*. Athens, GA: University of Georgia Press, 1982.

Lockwood, Charles. *Bricks and Brownstones: The New York Row House, 1783-1929*. New York: Abbeville Press, 1972.

Maas, John. *The Gingerbread Age*. New York: Bramhall House, 1952.

_____. *The Victorian Home in America*. New York: Hawthorn Books, 1972.

McAlester, Virginia and Lee. *A Field Guide to American Houses*. New York: Alfred E. Knopf, 1985.

McArdle, Alma deC and Deirdre with photographs by Frederick L. Hamilton. *Carpenter Gothic: Nineteenth-Century Ornamented Houses of New England*. New York: Whitney Library of Design/ Watson-Guptill, 1978.

Morrison, Mary L. (ed.) *Historic Savannah*. Historic Savannah Foundation, Junior League of Savannah, 1970.

Murphy, Thomas W., Jr. *The Wedding Cake House: The World of George W. Bourne*. Kennebunkport, Maine: Durrell Publications, 1978.

Myers, Denys Peter. *Maine Catalog: Historic American Buildings Survey*. Augusta: Maine State Museum, 1974.

Palliser, George and Charles. *The Pallisers' Late Victorian Architecture*: Introduction by Michael A. Tomlan. Watkins Glen: American Life Foundation, 1978.

Prokopoff, Steven S. and Siegfried, Joan C. with photographs by Joe Alper. *The Nineteenth-Century Architecture of Saratoga Springs*. New York State Council on the Arts, 1970.

Rubincam, Milton. "Mr. Christian Heurich and His Mansion." *Columbia Historical Society Records*, 1960-62.

Schumann, Marguerite E. *Grand Old Ladies: North Carolina Architecture During the Victorian Era*. Charlotte: Fast & McMillan Publishers, 1984.

Schwartz, Helen with photographs by Margaret Fisher. *The New Jersey House*. New Brunswick, N.J.: Rutgers University Press, 1983.

Sinclair, Peg B. with photographs by Taylor B. Lewis. *Victorious Victorians: A Guide to the Major Architectural Styles*. New York: Holt, Rhinehart and Winston, 1985.

Sloan, Samuel. *The Model Architect*. Philadelphia: E.G. Jones, 1852.

Thomas, George E. and Doebly, Carl. *Cape May: Queen of the Seaside Resorts*. Philadelphia: The Art Alliance Press, 1976.

Tolles, Bryant F. and Carolyn. *New Hampshire Architecture: An Illustrated Guide*. Hanover, N.H.: University Press of New England, 1979.

Wilson, Edmund. *Upstate: Records and Recollections of Northern New York*. New York: Farrar, Strauss & Giroux, 1971.

Wodehouse, Lawrence. *American Architects from the Civil War to the First World War*. Detroit: Gale Research, 1976.

Woodward, Wm. McKenzie and Sanderson, Edward F. *Providence: A Citywide Survey of Historic Resources*. Providence: Rhode Island Historical Preservation Commission, 1986.

Wrenn, Tony with photographs by W.E. Barrett. *Wilmington North Carolina: An Architectural and Historical Portrait*. Charlottesville: University Press of Virginia, 1984.

Wrobel, Arthur (ed.) *Pseudo-Science and Society in Nineteenth-Century America*. Lexington: University Press of Kentucky, 1987.

Zukowski, John. *Hudson River Villas*. New York: Rizzoli, 1985.

Unpublished Papers

Jaeger, A. Robert. "Historic Structure Survey Report: The Sprague House, Ithaca New York." For M.A. Tomlan, Cornell University, May, 1982. (Typewritten)

Kettlewell, James K. "The Batcheller Mansion." Skidmore College, Saratoga Springs, New York. Work in progress.

Medeiros, Peggi. "The Rotch Cottage." Office of Neighborhood & Historic Preservation, City of New Bedford, Massachusetts. 1981. (Typewritten)

Raymond, Allan. "The Story of Richfield Springs." Richfield Springs Historic District Association: Richfield Springs, New York. n.d. (Typewritten)

U.S. Department of Interior. National Park Service. "National Register of Historic Places. Inventory-Nomination Forms." Various dates, locations.

Index to Architects

Index to Houses

246